P9-DOG-598

Understanding Horses

Trafalgar Square Publishing
NORTH POMFRET VERMONT

TO

Rahalima, my horse who taught me to write; and Dr Ainslie Meares, my father, who encouraged me to do so.

First published in the United States of America in 1990 by Trafalgar Square Publishing. North Pomfret, Vermont 05053
Reprinted 1992

Library of Congress Catalog Number: 89–51605
ISBN 0 943955 20 3

Printed in Great Britain by Redwood Press Limited, Melksham, Wiltshire for Trafalgar Square Publishing

NOTES ON THE ILLUSTRATIONS

The photographs are of pure Arabian horses, with the obvious exceptions of the draught horse and pony. As the horses have been photographed to reveal an inward state of mind – rather than any outward grace or glamour – some of them shall remain nameless!

The names of the horses in the following illustrations are listed for the interest of the many owners and admirers of Arabian horses everywhere.

COVER *Halima Ivanhoe* (Rahalima^{+} [imp *USA*] × Inanna) stallion

FRONTISPIECE *Fahada* (Radstar × Lanwor Bon Abu) filly

2 *Quluah* (Radstar × Madibar) anglo-arab mare

3 *Tristram Yoni* (Tristram Selam × Bashqa) and her colt *El Sha'ir* (by Arabian Park Sabuh)

4 *Zanjabil*

6, 7, 8 *Rahalima*$^{+}$

9 *Bostocks Fantastique* (Sunshine Bey [imp USA] × Salila) mare
13 *Rahalima*⁺
19 *Dessertlite* (Sindh [imp UK] × Flash Lass) stallion
21 *Tristram Yoni* and her filly *El Halima* (by Rahalima⁺)
22 *Kharrubi* (Rahalima⁺ [imp USA] × Tristram Yoni) and *Halima Ivanhoe* as foals
23 *Halima Fire* (Rahalima⁺ [imp USA] × Firebird) colt
32 *Rahalima*⁺
33 *Quluah*
34 *Clarendon Wassan* (Clarendon Oramah × Wagga Jandowae) stallion
35 *Clarendon Wassan*
37 *Rahalima*⁺

CONTENTS

1

UNDERSTANDING HORSES - EARLIER ATTEMPTS

Throughout Man's long association with the Horse, the most successful horsemen have been those who have used some degree of knowledge of psychology or understanding of the horse, rather than trying to dominate the horse with force. Or, more simply, those people who are sensitive, perceptive, and sensible in relation to horses, and develop an empathy or a rapport with them, are the most effective with them.

The earliest story in history of the successful use of psychology to manage a horse, is that of Alexander the Great (356–323 BC) and Bucephalus.

Bucephalus was a tall, black Arabian stallion with a white star. He had been bred by the Thessalians who were the most renowned horse breeders of those times – their horses being famous over all others for their beauty, courage, speed, and endurance; and Bucephalus was one of the best! The owner of the horse, realising his value, and that a king would pay a handsome price for him, offered him for sale to King Philip II of Macedonia for the enormous sum of thirteen golden talents. However, when they went into the field to try him, he was vicious and unmanageable; and reared up when anyone endeavoured to mount him. Eventually the horse was led away as wholly useless and intractable.

Alexander, the King's son, who was at that time twelve years old, called out to his father: 'What an excellent horse do they lose for want of skill and courage to manage him!'

Philip at first took no notice of what he said; but when he heard him repeat the same thing several times, and saw he was greatly upset by the horse being sent away, eventually replied: 'Are you criticising those who are older than yourself, as if you knew more, and were better able to manage him than they?'

'I could manage this horse,' Alexander answered seriously, 'better than others do.'

'And if you do not,' retorted Philip impatiently, 'what will you forfeit for your rashness?'

'I will pay,' said Alexander with determination, 'the whole price of the horse.'

At this the whole company fell a-laughing, but Alexander ran to the horse and, taking hold of the bridle, turned him directly towards the sun. He had already noticed that the horse was frightened by the movement of his own shadow. He stroked the horse gently; then letting his cloak fall softly to the ground, with one leap securely mounted him. He paused a moment, and when he found that the horse was no longer rebellious, and only impatient to gallop, he let him go at full speed.

Philip and his friends looked on in silence and apprehension, until they saw Alexander turn back towards them at the end of the gallop, and return joyful and triumphant with his success. Immediately they all burst out into shouts of applause and praise.

Philip, with tears running down his face with relief and joy, kissed his son as he dismounted from the horse, and said: 'Oh my son, you must look for a kingdom equal to and worthy of yourself, for Macedonia is too little for you!'

Which is exactly what Alexander did.

Bucephalus became Alexander's constant companion for the next eighteen years, and Alexander rode Bucephalus in all the wars and campaigns that were to make his empire larger than any other that had ever preceded it.

Bucephalus eventually died of wounds at thirty years of age, in 326 BC, following Alexander's war with the Indian king, Porus.

Alexander was grieved to lose such a good friend, and built the city Bucephalia in memory of him. Alexander himself died only three years later.[1]

The ancient Greeks were good horsemen – they had to be. Horses were ridden bareback, without the advantage of stirrups or saddle, and the riders were more dependent upon ability than on equipment.

So, it is unsurprising that some of the most important writing on horsemanship dates from this era.

In 400 BC, Xenophon, a Greek general and writer, wrote his book *Peri Hippikes* or 'On Horsemanship'. To this book 'must be given the credit for preserving the ideas of equestrian art to the present day, because it was this book that formed the basis of its renaissance'.[2] (After the fall of the Greek Empire, the knowledge of many arts, including the art of horsemanship, gradually disappeared and did not re-emerge until the sixteenth century.)

Xenophon's training of horses was based on commonsense and kindness, and understanding the psychology of the horse. He says:

When a horse is shy of any object, and reluctant to approach it, the rider must try to make him feel that there is nothing terrible in it, especially to a horse of spirit; but if he cannot succeed, the rider must himself touch that which appears so alarming, and lead the horse up gently to it.

As to those who force horses forward with blows in such a case, they only inspire them with greater terror; for they imagine, when they suffer any pain at such a time, that what they look upon with alarm is in some way the cause of it.[3]

Xenophon's teachings are best summed up by the following statements:

We however consider it the best mode of instruction, as we are perpetually saying, that when ever a horse acts agreeably to the wishes of his rider, it should follow that he receive some indulgence from him. For what a horse does under compulsion . . . he does without understanding, and with no more grace than a dancer would display if a person should whip and spur him during his performance . . .

This we may express, indeed, in a few words, but it should influence us throughout all our treatment of horses; for a horse will more readily take the bit, if, when he has taken it, something pleasant results to himself; and he will leap across ditches, and jump over obstacles, and comply with our wishes in all other respects, if he looks forward, when he has done what is required of him, to some indulgence.[4]

It should be remembered that Xenophon was no weak sentimentalist, but a highly skilled and successful military commander. Hence he says: 'A servant and an army, if disobedient, are useless, but a disobedient horse is not only useless, but often plays the traitor.'

The Roman Empire eventually swamped that of the Greeks, coarsening and debasing all its art forms. People ceased trying to understand the psychology of the horse, and cruel methods of training were used based on force and pain. Xenophon's methods disappeared.

Then, with the Renaissance in the sixteenth century, interest in the art of riding and horsemanship reappeared.

A Neopolitan nobleman, Federico Grisone, studied Xenophon's books concerning horses; and as a result of this he not only opened a riding academy where young noblemen, including the sons of many European kings and princes, were tutored in the arts of handling horses and courtly behaviour; but he also published, in 1550, his book *Ordini di Cavalcare*, of which much had been copied from Xenophon's works. Unlike Xenophon, however, Grisone advocated the use of extreme punishment, violence, and brute force.

Grisone and his Neopolitan School were extremely influential, and his style of 'horsemanship' and use of extremely cruel curb bits spread throughout Europe, and eventually to the Americas with the early settlers.

Grisone's most famous pupil was Giovanni Pignatelli. He became the director of the Riding Academy at Naples and taught the Frenchman, Antoine de Pluvinel.

Pluvinel in turn, in 1594, opened his own academy in Paris, where young men, including his famous pupil, the young Louis XIII, came to learn not only dressage riding, but, in the spirit of the times, painting, dancing, and fencing as well.

Pluvinel was the first riding master to oppose the cruel methods in use by his contempories. Following the fall of the Greek Empire, riding masters had used very rough methods. They did not even try to make their horses do what they wanted by the ordinary or commonplace methods of these days; they believed that punishment was the best method of education, and this style of 'horsemanship' persisted into the seventeenth century and beyond.

Pluvinel regarded all horses as individuals, and recognised that their temperaments can differ greatly. He advocated less harsh methods of training, and the use of kindness rather than force.

At first Pluvinel's radical ideas were ridiculed, but after his death in 1622, and the publication of his book

L'Instruction du Roi the following year, his methods were gradually accepted.

These new principles of greater kindness towards horses continued, despite the many advocates of cruel practices which were recommended not only by the Neopolitan School but also by other influential writers on the Continent and in England.

At the beginning of the eighteenth century, France became the nation with the greatest influence in the art of riding and horsemanship. In 1733, the great riding master Francois Robichon de la Guérinière, who was master of horse to King Louis XV of France, produced his book *Ecole de Cavalerie*. His teachings were regarded as being of such importance that they are used unaltered to this day at the Spanish Riding School in Vienna. It is this School which has continued to influence, both directly and indirectly, the best dressage riders and instructors of the present time.

Alois Podhajsky, a former director of the Spanish Riding School, in his book *The Complete Training of Horse and Rider in the Principles of Classical Horsemanship* (1973), remarks that 'Pluvinel and Guérinière had many followers who influenced teaching throughout the years that followed. This not only saved the art of riding, but proved of great benefit to the horse.'[5]

Podhajsky has the easy, intuitive, commonsense approach of the natural horseman. He stresses the importance of reward, and mentions different ways of praising the horse: 'The simplest way for the rider to show his appreciation is by patting or speaking with a soothing voice. Patting does not mean slapping the horse with the open hand to make as much noise as possible, which is often done to impress the onlookers; the horse's neck should be caressed fondly and delicately.'[6]

Additionally, he abhors the misuse of punishment, and emphasises that the punishment must be just, and the horse must understand why it is being punished. He observes that 'the rider with high ambitions and little knowledge will be more inclined to revert to punishment than will the more experienced rider. He will try to obtain by force what he cannot achieve by the correct use of the aids as taught by the classical school.'[7]

However, Podhajsky's book is very much concerned with technique, and his few references to understanding the mind of the horse – such as the importance of not hurting or frightening a young horse, and the value of using the horse's herd instinct during its initial training – are virtually swamped by details of the art of correct riding.

Other modern horsemen, too, have produced perceptive horse books, without exploring the mind and emotions of the horse. The successful rider and breeder, Henry Wynmalen[8], through his kind and intuitive approach to the handling and management of horses, has no doubt been of tremendous influence in England, Australia, and New Zealand, in reinforcing humane and commonsense ways of caring for and training horses, and in illustrating the greater pleasure and success produced by using such methods.

This gradual increase in kindness and humanity towards horses has paralleled peoples' increasing consideration of other people and the education and treatment of children. In the centuries where children were treated like Oliver Twist and worse; where children were beaten, half-starved, and put to work for sixteen hours a day and more; it is not surprising that horses were treated no better.

The growth of humanitarianism brought with it not only concern for the individual, but an increasing interest in the functioning of the human mind and unconscious thought. It even became possible to consider that the horse might also have a mind!

James Fillis was a riding master of the last century who

captivated large audiences with his over-bent horses with unnatural gaits. People were very impressed by horses which could canter on three legs, and even canter backwards! Fillis's training methods were cruel, and fortunately were quickly forgotten after his death, but he is of interest because he tried to demonstrate (although unsuccessfully) how horses think.

> Fillis did not like horses. He declared contemptuously that their only well-developed mental quality was their memory, that they only had a small amount of intelligence, and that they were 'incapable of affection for man.'
>
> This 'lack of affection for man' he decided to prove experimentally. However, due to his lack of perception, he made an incorrect conclusion.
>
> Fillis fed sugar and carrots to horses belonging to other people, and was convinced that the horses lacked affection for their owners because they started whinnying to him after a number of visits with the food. He concluded that the horses were whinnying to him through affection. He did not realise that they had learnt to expect food from him, and were simply shouting: 'I want my dinner!'

There has been very little work done on the psychology of the horse. Most studies consider only social behaviour in the herd, or readily observed facts, such as that the horse is easily frightened, or that it will work better if it is rewarded rather than punished. It is then quite understandable that the blurb to John Clabby's *The Natural History of the Horse* (1976) can claim the book incorporates 'the results of the latest researches in the growing science of ethology'. In fact it incorporates only very superficial observations.

> It seems that the calls [of horses] are highly individual and mothers and foals in particular can recognize and respond to one another's voice. Some calls have a more general effect, for instance a loud neigh or whinny may alarm the whole herd . . . in the main however, so far as communications between individuals are concerned, visual signals are more important than sounds. Horses have a quick eye for slight muscular movements and changes in the posture of their companions and perhaps communicate many of their feelings by signalling in some such subliminal manner. To the human eye horses use five distinctly different facial expressions to suit different circumstances.[9]

These are the faces of threat, greeting, submission, yawning, and the Flehman posture.

In 1976, Henry Blake published the first of a number of books that showed that he had studied the horse's mind in depth. In his first book, *Talking With Horses*, he even went to the extent of compiling a dictionary of horse vocabulary![10]

Blake noticed that people used more than words when they communicated with each other, and realised that horses did the same. He found that 'language, in short, was not a question of sounds only – it was a whole complex of verbal and non-verbal communication, some of it highly individual and dependent on familiarity for its comprehension.[11] Each horse has its own individual language, and the same meaning can be expressed in a number of different ways.

Blake says: 'In learning to interpret the horse's vocal sounds, the tone, note and delivery are all to be taken into account, and so are the non-verbal messages – the body signs – that accompany the sound.' So if the horse raised the note of the whinny when it was demanding its food, the message would change from 'I want my dinner', to (according to Blake): 'Where is my bloody breakfast, you fool, I'm starving.'

Blake's researches showed that there are some thirty or

so basic messages which are used by the domestic horse, and there are another seventeen phrases that are used occasionally or in special situations, for example, those messages between a mare and her foal, or a stallion and a mare. He also lists fifty-four sub-messages.

Additionally, he found that when a horse discovered that the messages it was trying to convey were understood, either by another horse or by a person, its range of communication could be extended considerably. If a wild and untouched horse was stabled with a domestic one that vocally demanded food, the wild horse would learn the domesticated horse's vocabulary in a very short time and be whinnying for its breakfast too. Out of one hundred and twenty-two horses, only three had not learned to ask for food within seven days.

Blake also realised that, although horses have an extensive body language as well, there was still a much greater degree of communication between horses, and between himself and horses, than could be explained by sounds and signs.

He became convinced that the horses were sensing his moods and feelings and were anticipating his wishes through telepathy, and he proved its existence by using pairs of closely bonded or empathic horses (horses who were mentally and emotionally close to each other) in a series of experiments.

More than this, he even showed that horses use clairvoyance – the ability to see mentally something that exists or is happening out of sight – but to a much lesser degree.

Blake says that the use of clairvoyance would seem to be a skill beyond the ordinary person. It 'is the most difficult form of communication to learn, though since it is used only to a very limited extent, the skill is not essential to the handling of horses'. Interestingly he adds: 'It is easy to identify what animal you are receiving the [clairvoyant] message from, since he won't be in the picture you are receiving.'

Blake believed that if he could understand all aspects of his horses, he could make them happy and motivate them to work better and to be more successful in competition.

In contrast, there are unfortunately still many followers of the harsh Neopolitan School to be found, especially on the Continent and in the USA. Like Grisone, they believe that the horse regards it as a reward when the rider or handler stops punishing it!

Recently a 'successful' horseperson came from the USA to judge at a major Australian show and to give a seminar on training horses.[12] Horses were trained on the principle of education by punishment: a cut of the cane or chin-chain for every incorrect step, movement, or look. They became motivated to do what the trainer wished through fear of repeated pain. It was even demonstrated how to load a foal into a horse float by making everywhere so 'unpleasant' for the foal, that the horse float became the only refuge and release from pain! Unsurprisingly, this trainer announced that: 'The greatest reward you can give your horse is not to touch it!'

Such harsh methods are not only cruel and completely unnecessary, but they destroy the horse. The use of the severe cane and chain treatment on one of the above demonstration horses produced a splendid performance in the show ring; but it also reduced a friendly, confident, and willing filly into a permanently sulky, anxious, and distrustful horse.

It has been shown time and time again that, if we follow the path of kindness and understanding begun by Xenophon, there is a more successful and gratifying way of training horses – as illustrated so long ago by Alexander the Great with his charger Bucephalus.

2

THE NEEDS OF THE HORSE

What makes horses 'tick'? What makes them think and function in the way they do? Learning the needs of horses is the first step in discovering their emotions, and understanding their behaviour.

Horses, like people, have a number of essential needs, both physical and psychological.

Their physical needs are for food, water, shelter from extreme weather, a safe environment, sensory stimulation, light, exercise, and freedom from injury, pain, or parasites. Essential psychological needs are for companionship of other horses, affection, self-esteem, respect and acceptance by the herd, mental stimulation, and sufficient space.

Domesticated horses, again like people, can be conditioned to have other needs too, and can learn to like or want something which would be of no interest to a wild horse. So a horse can learn, or be conditioned, to need the affection and approval of people, for example, or have the desire to achieve and win races instilled in it.

The physical needs of horses

Some of the essential physical needs of horses have been covered at length by numerous other books, so will only be briefly mentioned. It goes without saying, of course, that neglecting a horse's physical needs will damage or undermine a horse's health, and consequently its well-being and how it feels in itself.

Horses need sufficient good feed, and due to the extremely long length of their intestines they need a lot of roughage – that means good pasture or hay. If they do not have enough hay or pasture they are liable to get intestinal problems, sometimes caused by eating inappropriate or unwholesome substances such as fence posts or mouldy hay. Additionally, a lot of poor quality hay or grass will only give them a huge belly, and little flesh over the ribs and along the spine.

Good pastures are normally sown, and consist of rye grass, clovers, and possibly timothy or some other suitable grasses. Native grasses usually have insufficient nutritional value as they provide considerably less protein. Even if a paddock or field is green and appears to be thickly covered, the grasses or weeds may be unsuitable and unpalatable for horses – especially if the ground lacks drainage, and the grass is rank and sour. Also, horses will not eat around their own manure unless they are actually starving.

There is something quite special about good green grass. Some horses that are well fed on hay and grain all through the dry months of summer may never have a real glow of health until the spring grasses appear. Horses always seem to prefer good green pasture to hay, and it is in fact higher in vitamins and protein than all hays except for lucerne. Therefore it is not surprising that those horses and ponies that are likely to become overweight and founder, are especially likely to do so in the spring.

However, good spring grasses rapidly turn into dry stringy fibre with low vitamin and protein value under the heat of the summer sun, and most horses will need supplementary feeding, irrespective of how large their paddock is.

Good meadow hay consists of the same grasses and clovers as a good pasture. It should be free of weeds or seeds that are poisonous or can damage a horse's mouth, such as barley grass. Good hay should also smell good, have retained its green colour, and be free of dust and mould. Hay that has lost its colour has a lower nutritional value and is less palatable. If hay has been rained on it may be completely useless.

The best test of hay is to buy a bale before you buy a truck-load, and to try it out on your horse or horses. If they don't like it, you will have to try some other hay instead.

Lucerne is much better than all other hays nutritionally and for palatability. It is considerably higher in protein, calcium, and vitamins, than any other hay. When it is necessary to feed hay out to horses, it is preferable that they should get at least one fifteen to twenty centimetre biscuit of lucerne hay a day in addition to their other hay. In spite of the number of old wives tales about lucerne, it can be fed as the only hay to a horse, and in fact it is often preferable to do so.

Ponies usually don't need very much supplementary feeding; but larger horses, stallions, brood mares, young stock, and working horses, will all need extra food in the form of grain – especially during winter and late summer when there is very little good natural feed available.

Oats are the safest and most natural grain to give to horses; they have been part of the development of the horse over the last two thousand years. If grain is fed to a horse it is essential to add a calcium supplement. Grains have a calcium-phosphorus imbalance, and if calcium is not added to horses' food, it is leached from their bones instead. This deficiency is frequently obvious in foals whose dams have not been fed sufficient calcium, and the foals may have dramatic leg defects as a result. Mature horses are likely to suffer a softening of the bones due to the demineralisation, which can predispose them to other problems.

The calcium-phosphorus (Ca:P) imbalance is considerably lower in oats, being about 1:3, than that in barley or corn (being 1:6 and 1:11 respectively). Nevertheless, it is still necessary to feed out calcium with oats, as the phosphorus level should not be higher than that of calcium. Ideally, the ratio of calcium to phosphorus should be about 2 parts of calcium to 1 of phosphorus, and at its very lowest 1:1. An imbalance with a Ca:P as close as 1:1.6 causes problems to occur rapidly. Although no troubles seem to occur from excess calcium; if both calcium *and phosphorus* levels are high, damage can result.[13]

The best forms of oats to feed horses, especially the very young or old, are possibly 'steamed and rolled' or 'bruised' oats. Whole oats need to be fed in a larger quantity, as a proportion of them tend to pass undigested through the horse; and crushed oats are usually smashed into oblivion, and reduced to a poor quality feed of husks and dust.

Veterinary surgeons point out the problems associated with feeding horses too much grain. These include the risks of developing splints, joint damage due to overweight in young horses, founder, and azoturia in working horses. However, some horses require a lot of grain, like brood mares and working horses, and their feed needs to be carefully and knowledgeably managed.

Frequently, horses appear fat to the casual observer because they have a large belly. However, very often they are not fat at all; the horses are actually thin and out of shape due to malnutrition and possibly parasites. Such horses often have a very long coat of hair, a 'malnutrition coat', which the horse grows against cold, as it does not have the normal layer of fat under its skin to protect it.

A horse in good condition should have a flat back, even a 'double spine' or 'tiger spine' (where the flesh and muscle is raised on each side of the spine in two ridges); the rump should be rounded; and the ribs well-covered and not visible to the eye. However, if the ribs cannot be felt at all, the horse is too fat.

Some of a horse's physical needs can also dramatically influence its temperament; this is especially true with feed. A horse that is underfed is likely to be dull and lethargic; whereas an overfed horse which has too little exercise, especially if it is fed grain, is likely to be over-excited and silly.

Horses have a need to chew, and a diet that provides sufficient pasture or hay will satisfy this need. In a recent widespread drought, when all pastures were eaten bare and it was very difficult to obtain hay, a large number of horses were maintained in good condition on grain but received only half their normal ration of hay. As a consequence, the horses chewed not only every stem and root out of their paddocks, but chewed the trees and fence posts as well.

Horses need ample fresh water, which means keeping water troughs clean and filled; and making sure that ground water, such as in dams or streams, does not become polluted.

Troughs should not be placed in the very corner of paddocks or yards. They should be placed where horses can have free access to them without the fear of being trapped and hurt by a more aggressive horse higher in the pecking order.

It is essential to provide shelter for horses to protect them from the extremes of heat, cold, wind, or rain. (It is also preferable to rug them in cold or wet weather, but they need to be under daily supervision in case the rug slips.) A desirable size for a shelter shed is about four by four metres, and closed on three sides. Its back should be towards the most prevailing winds – probably the west, so the shed is open on its east side. Shelter trees are also desirable, especially in the summer.

In hilly country, horses always like to spend some of each day on the tops of the hills: they need to satisfy their desire for the space and freedom that a hilltop provides. So, if they are paddocked lower on a hillside, they frequently wear a track with restless pacing along the highest fence – rather than along any other. For this reason, if shelter sheds are placed in a paddock, they may have to be placed at the top of the hill and preferably near the gate. Horses tend not to use badly sited shelter sheds, no matter how hot or cold it is.

When horses are put together in paddocks, they need to be carefully chosen for their mutual compatibility. In fact, it is desirable that they should meet and get to know each other for a day or two over a safe fence (possibly a mesh that a horse can't kick a leg through) before they are put in with each other. Horses in groups have a very definite pecking order, and a safe getting-to-know-you-period can help prevent fighting, kicks, bites, and damaged horses.

A small group of horses in a paddock, perhaps three or four individuals, is more satisfactory than a large group. In a small group there is less stress to the horses, especially those lower in the hierarchy, and it is also safer and more pleasant for the people handling and feeding them.

Obviously stallions and colts over ten months old need special arrangements, and brood mares and foals should have a paddock of their own; but sometimes other horses can be very aggressive. Occasionally a gelding, or even a mare, may be so aggressive that there is a real possibility of it seriously injuring another horse, especially if there are shelter sheds another horse can be trapped in, although for some horses even the corner of the paddock is enough.

As we have already mentioned, for this reason, shelter sheds and troughs are never placed in the very corners of paddocks or yards.

It is normal not only for stallions to seek mares, but for a mare when she comes into season to seek a stallion. Some mares will actually stand and paw at a paddock fence because they want to get to a stallion that is a couple of paddocks away – consequently they are likely to cut a leg or rip off a shoe if the bottom wire of the fence is too close to the ground. Mares usually enjoy the company of a stallion, even when they are not in season, unless through a bad stud experience they have learnt to fear them.

Geldings can often be very unpredictable in their behaviour towards other horses, and can sometimes be a problem paddocked with mares. Some may be docile, whereas others can be very aggressive and bossy towards all other horses, and a few may even mount mares that come into season. Some geldings will 'tease' mares, and so can be a danger if on the other side of a wire fence, as a mare may strike out or kick at the gelding and injure herself in the fence.

The degree of a gelding's aggressiveness appears to be governed more by heredity, rather than at what age he was castrated. However, it is completely unreasonable to expect a male horse which has learnt the social behaviour of a stallion to completely change its habits, behaviour, and personality because it is castrated. A castrated stallion who has been used at stud may continue to behave like an entire, but be infertile. Young stallions who have never served a mare may settle down after castration, but a good six months may be needed to allow for the hormones to leave their system. In general, it is best to geld a colt before he is one-year old.

It is difficult to make a horse's environment completely safe. Paddocks should never have acute angles or corners of less than ninety degrees, where a horse may become trapped by others; fences should never have barbed wire or cattle mesh in them. If fences are made of plain wire, the lowermost strand should be about 14in (35cm) from the ground. Horses put their feet over low wires all too easily, especially when they are trying to eat the grass on the other side of the fence. Then, when they try and step back they find that their leg is caught. Most horses panic, and then they can inflict terrible damage upon themselves.

Mares on the point of foaling should not be in a paddock where fencing does not reach the ground, as the newborn foal may arrive on the other side of the fence! Needless to say, mares should never be left to foal in paddocks with dams, creeks, ravines, or other hazards. Many foals die, not only from injuries, but from drowning.

Although it is desirable to rotate horse paddocks and to have cows grazing them too, it is not always successful having horses and cows together at the same time. Stallions, colts, and geldings tend to be rather mean to cows and other animals; they enjoy chasing them relentlessly, and some have a special obsession for chewing the ears of cattle.

Such 'anti-social' behaviour is related to a horse's great need for sensory and mental stimulation. A horse needs to be able to use its different senses of sight, hearing, touch, smell, and taste, and to perceive change and variety. A horse lacking in sensory stimulation (not necessarily a need to chase or chew cows!) is likely to become very depressed or anxious, will possibly go off its food, and even become ill. If the deprivation lasts too long, the horse may suffer from impaired physical and intellectual ability, together with emotional and behavioural vices and problems.

Visual stimulation and variety is especially important. When puppies for research were raised in isolation in a laboratory, it was noticed that the ill-effects of such rearing could be somewhat offset by cutting a window into the side of their box so that they could see out into the busy laboratory. Giving the puppies a companion, or playthings, failed to have such a beneficial effect.[14]

It would seem that the growing tendency towards stabling horses all day inside barns or sheds, where their visual stimulation is dramatically reduced, is likely to produce increasing numbers of overanxious or fearful horses, who behave inappropriately in the outside world.

Closely connected to a horse's need for sensory stimulation is its need for exercise.

> Sometimes when it is really cold, and it rains heavily all day long, some of the horses that we normally stable overnight are kept in longer, and may not be put out in the paddock until the next day when the rain has stopped. Somehow we expect them to be happy to be kept in a place which is warm and dry, where they can eat to their heart's content with their companions; but no, they become quite upset. When at last they are released, they are positively maniacal, and gallop and buck around the paddock twice as much as usual before settling down to eating the grass.

Horses need to exercise each day, for both their physical and psychological welfare. A horse that is kept in a stable or small yard, and is not exercised, is likely to become a poor-moving physical specimen, and may even develop permanent physical damage such as contracted tendons. Additionally, the horse's temperament is likely to deteriorate dramatically, and the horse may become not only more difficult to manage, but may also develop some vice, such as viciousness, wind-sucking, cribbing, weaving, or biting its own body and tearing its own skin.

Sometimes horses that are kept in such unacceptable conditions and are not exercised, which is frequently the fate of stallions, develop other forms of behaviour, in compensation, which are more socially acceptable.

Moz was a four-year old stallion who for most of his life, the three and a half years following weaning, had been kept in a small yard measuring no more than 20 × 20ft (6 × 6m). As a consequence of lacking adequate space to move, he could not walk, trot, or canter correctly. However, he managed to keep a certain degree of sanity by exercising himself in regular bucking sessions at about four o'clock every afternoon.

Moz was eventually sold to a new home where he was kept in a paddock. Several months passed before he forgot to have his daily bucking session, and learnt the simple art of cantering instead.

However, even after several years, his paces never regained the natural, easy, long-stepping flow they had had as a paddocked youngster; and his personality could be kindly described as awkward, and certainly wasn't to be trusted.

Horses have a need for movement: they are rarely still. Even horses that appear to be asleep or resting, continue to change their weight from one hind foot to the other, to swish their tails, twitch an occasional muscle in their sides, and to keep their ears moving and informing them of what is happening all around.

The horse's need for movement and exercise is a result of the evolutionary process. Thousands of years ago, horses were grazing dinners for the carnivores which stalked them through the grasslands, and the horses which survived were the fittest, fastest, strongest, and most alert.

Another requirement of horses, which we often don't consider, is the need for light. In nature there is no completely dark situation, unless one is under the ground! So complete darkness can cause panic.

Horses that have been transported in dark closed-in horse trucks, certainly learn to fear them. Whereas the same horses often travel quite happily in the ordinary, well-lighted, double horse trailers drawn by a car.

Horses nearly always hesitate when they are led into a dark stable at night, even if they know their dinner is ready and waiting for them there. If horses are to be housed indoors, faint illumination at night is preferable, and a shielded twenty-five watt electric light can be arranged to give about the same amount of illumination as a nearly full moon. Accidents more commonly occur in dark stables than those that have a glimmer of light.

Horses also require other health care. They need attention to their hooves, regular treatment for internal parasites (and sometimes external parasites), and dental checks.

Even if a horse is not ridden or worked, its hooves must be regularly maintained; otherwise they are likely to badly deteriorate, and as the old saying goes: 'No foot, no horse!'

Horses' feet need to be trimmed, preferably by a farrier, every six or eight weeks. If the hooves are allowed to grow too long there is excessive strain on the tendons and lameness can result. Feet that grow unevenly, or become broken, can also cause strain on a horse's legs, and can cause permanent damage in young horses. If the horse is worked, or the feet wear too short, the horse may have to be shod about every six weeks.

Sometimes the heel on the foot wears less than the toe and sides, so that the frog becomes raised above the ground, and the heel becomes contracted, and the pastern upright. The heel should be trimmed so that the frog comes into contact with the ground. This contact creates a pumping action which stimulates correct blood circulation in the foot.

All horses are likely to suffer from internal parasites or 'worms' and should be regularly treated for them. *Strongyles* or 'blood worms', *ascarids* or 'round worms', and bots are the most common.

Strongyles, or 'blood' or 'red worms', damage blood vessels, and are a common cause of fatal colics since they affect the blood supply to the intestines.

The larvae of red worms crawl up the blades of grass and are eaten by horses. The larvae then penetrate the intestinal wall, and travel through the horse's tissues to organs such as the liver and pancreas. Larvae may also be picked up by the bloodstream and carried to other organs; and some might reach the anterior mesenteric artery, which is the main source of blood to the intestines. They cause damage to the vessel lining, which then creates a tendency for blood clots or emboli to develop. These emboli are likely to totally block the small capillaries that supply the intestines. The intestinal wall, deprived of nutrients, becomes necrotic and ceases to function. Death of the horse is a common outcome.

Ascarids, or large roundworms, are very common in young horses, but do not seem to appear in those over five years old. Ascarids are particularly damaging. Because of their large size and numbers (they can look very much like a large serving of spaghetti!), they can completely obstruct an intestine. Additionally, they migrate through the tissues of the horse, especially the liver and lungs, and cause considerable damage.

Bots are the larvae of a fly. The flies lay their eggs mostly on the hairs of the horse's legs, where they hatch and enter the horse's mouth when it scratches itself. The larvae then migrate through the tissue of the mouth (cheeks, tongue, and pharynx) to the stomach, where they attach themselves to the stomach lining.

Consequently, all horses must be regularly wormed.

If a horse is not eating normally, and there is no known cause, its teeth should be checked.

Horse's teeth grow throughout their lives, and are continually worn by chewing. Sometimes sharp points develop on the edges of the teeth which will lacerate the tongue or the inside of the cheek. Naturally the horse will be discouraged from eating. A veterinary surgeon's services will be necessary to file the teeth correctly.

As we have seen, there are many aspects that will affect the physical condition of the horse, and which in turn will play a very important part in the health and functioning of the horse's mind.

The psychological needs of horses

Horses have a number of psychological needs, too, and if these are not satisfied the horse is likely to become anxious or depressed. It might lose condition and become mentally unbalanced, or even ill.

Of course a horse's physical needs have to be satisfied to avoid psychological distress too. If a horse is left unfed one day, it will feel the physical stress of lack of food and be hungry and lose condition, and it will also suffer anxiety caused by the hunger which will cause it to lose additional weight.

Anxiety caused by lack of food or some other essential need is an innate response in every animal. It forces it into trying to satisfy the need which is necessary for its physical survival. Hence, a hungry horse will seek food. However, many domestic horses have been conditioned to expect food from people. So, although a wild horse would continually roam in search of food, a domestic horse may not, or may not have the opportunity to do so.

Consequently, some horses will go down in the paddock and eat more grass, others will walk or canter up and down the fence endlessly expecting their food, while others will call, 'I want my dinner!', or strike at their stable doors, or paw at the fencing. In contrast, some may go into a stupor of depression, or become so anxious that colic sets in. The psychological stress aggravates the physical stress upon the horse.

So, a horse's psychological needs include the ease of mind produced by satisfaction of its physical requirements; the need for companionship with another horse or horses; affection; self-satisfaction or self-esteem; respect and acceptance from the other members of the herd; sensory stimulation; and sufficient space – not only space large enough to canter in, but visual, psychological space.

One of the cruellest things people can do to a horse is to keep it by itself without contact with another horse. Horses are herd animals. Even the horse that appears to be a loner needs the herd. A solitary horse, if given the chance, will always try and join others.

People sometimes put other companion animals with a horse for company, like a sheep or cow. Solitary people often have a cat or dog as a companion too; but it is not the same as having a companion of one's own kind.

Horses need to belong to a herd for many related but completely separate reasons. Indeed, a large part of a horse's psychological wellbeing is dependent on it being part of a herd, or at least having the companionship of one or two others.

Other horses provide security. They help ward off the horse's instinctive perpetual fear of danger. They will share the vigil for tigers in every bush, and fire in every breath of wind. And if the herd is threatened, they will gallop off together or maybe huddle together, touching each other for reassurance.

The horse also needs companions to give and receive affection, to satisfy a need for belonging and being accepted by its own species, to develop self-esteem, to increase its sensory stimulation, and to develop the social skills and forms of communication necessary for a normal horse.

The horse has a basic and essential need for affection;

both to give and to receive it. The foal receives affection from its mother from the day it is born; and the bond is strengthened as the mare provides not only nourishment, but also contact, security, reassurance, and grooming sessions.

After a few weeks the foal gains sufficient confidence to start establishing friendships with other foals, and as the weeks pass it will spend more time with them, and less with its mother – unless it is frightened, and then it will dash back to her side for security and reassurance.

The foals will play together, eat grass together, sleep together, and enjoy just being together: they develop affection for each other. Then as the foal matures, it will form friendships with other horses and develop affection for them too.

Psychologists used to think that the affection-love bond that a baby has for its mother is based on the fact that the mother provides food and satisfies the infant's hunger drive. However, it has been shown that this is not the case. It is now known that contact and reassurance are more important than food in providing bonds of attachment and affection.[15,16]

If, for some reason (like recent starvation), a mare cannot provide milk for its newborn foal, and a person should feed the foal, the mare and foal still develop deep bonds of affection providing they are kept together.

Gradually, the mother's psychological importance to the foal lessens, and the company of horses of a similar age becomes more important.

In the spring, this need of young animals for the company of those of the same age is very obvious. Not only foals seek other foals for companions, but groups of calves and lambs can also be seen together in the paddocks, while the mothers graze further afield.

The foal receives not only affection and security from its mother, but also acceptance. Mares, on the whole, are surprisingly tolerant of the roughness and rudeness of their own offspring, and rarely seem to reprimand them, and if so, then perhaps with only a slight nip. So the foal will be naturally friendly and confident with its companions, and will be accepted by them.

The foal becomes a social animal and part of the herd, and as it matures it is likely to take a similar place in the social hierarchy of the herd as its mother. There are two reasons for this. Firstly, the foal learns to behave like its mother, and to be bossy or passive towards the various other horses; and secondly, and perhaps most importantly, because the foal is seen as part of its mother. Other mares will tolerate, boss, or defer to it as they would to the mother herself. The young horse quickly learns its position in society and gains acceptance from the other members of the herd as a whole.

The position of a horse in the social hierarchy of the herd will also relate to a horse's self-esteem. Horses at the top of the pecking order will have the highest self-esteem, and those at the bottom the lowest.

A horse's more or less inherited position in the herd can be altered by unusual conditions. An exceptionally aggressive horse may reduce the position of another natural herd leader; a racehorse that always comes last may slide down the social scale; whereas a horse low in self-esteem and of a more passive and gentle nature, may, if its confidence is given a considerable boost, decide to dominate other horses formerly higher in the pecking order. Frequently, horses that form a close bond with their riders have such a rise in self-esteem.

It is easy to see how the company of other horses satisfies so many essential needs. So it is not surprising that some solitary horses will go to extreme lengths to join other horses; even though the other horses may be quite unfriendly. The strange horse will hover around on the outskirts of the herd until it is eventually accepted.

There are a number of other less obvious reasons why the companionship of other horses is so important. Other horse companions are necessary for the young horse to develop the social skills and forms of communication necessary for a normal horse. They also increase the amount of sensory stimulation it receives.

A young horse that is reared without the company of others is likely to be socially inept with others as a mature horse: those reared on their own, such as orphan or solitary foals, are likely to learn inappropriate behaviour for their species.

Horses raised in isolation sometimes behave inappropriately towards potential sexual partners. Instead of 'getting on with the job', as the horsemen say, a colt or stallion may respond to the mare with fear, aggression, or playfulness – behaviour which normal animals display towards strange or novel objects. Isolating stallions from other horses obviously plays a large part in the aggression and even viciousness some stallions display towards mares. Mares, reared by themselves, may react to the stallion also with fear or aggression; and even if they are in season, they may refuse to respond to a stallion's overtures.

Horses kept in isolation, often the fate of colts after weaning, frequently display the inappropriate behaviour and high anxiety which is demonstrated time and time again in laboratory animals reared in impoverished environments with reduced mental and sensory stimulation.[17] Horses kept in small yards by themselves develop repetitive patterns of abnormal behaviour, such as whirling in circles and chasing their tails. Some horses indulge in this self-orientated activity by biting their own sides or legs, even to the extent of tearing their own flesh so that they bleed.

Other repetitive abnormal behaviour exhibited by deprived horses includes swinging the head and neck up and down, or from side to side, and the extension of this habit into the stable vice of weaving. The weaving horse not only swings its head and neck, but also the front end of its body from side to side. Deprived horses can also develop the stable vices of cribbing and wind-sucking. The crib-biter grips a fixed object with its teeth, arches its neck, and swallows air. It makes at the same time a characteristic noise that sounds like a burp. The wind-sucker is similar to the crib-biter, but manages to swallow air without latching on to any object so the teeth do not suffer abnormal and excessive wear.

It has been reported that isolation-reared laboratory animals show abnormal behaviour towards painful sensory stimulation, such as a burning match or pin-prick.[18] Their response was lower than that of control animals. It appears that the high level of anxiety created by entering a totally new environment, where everything was strange and unknown, interfered with the animal's ability to perceive genuine threats and to avoid them. Puppies that could formerly avoid electric shocks, were unable to perform the avoidance responses after several months of isolation-rearing.

The same is true with horses. If a horse is continually kept in a boring or impoverished environment, and is then moved to another environment, *watch out*! So much will be strange to it; strange sights, strange sounds, strange everything. It will receive so many previously unknown stimuli that it will not be able to cope with the flood of messages it is receiving. The horse's brain will not be able to sort out the messages, to integrate them, and respond appropriately to them. The horse will be unpredictable, and from the handler's point of view it may be downright dangerous!

Horses need to be able to use their different senses of sight, hearing, touch, smell, and taste, and to perceive change and variety.

All these senses are much easier to satisfy in the paddocked horse than in the stabled horse. This is especially true if the stables are in a shed or barn. The horse stabled in a shed or barn cannot see people, cars, and animals come and go; or a cat or dog wandering by, birds flying, the wind in the grass and trees, and so on. Nor can the horse hear so much when stabled, although some people try and overcome this deficiency by leaving a radio playing all day in the stable for the horse's benefit. The stabled horse cannot touch as much as the paddocked horse, nor can it scratch or have any reassuring contact with a companion. Smell, too, is limited, probably to what is kept in the barn: horses, feed, manure, leather, and perhaps motor oil. And taste may be more limited too.

Additionally, barn conditions can be very static, so that every day is the same. Horses need to be able to perceive change and variety through their senses; especially visually. They also need physical change in routine to provide mental stimulation, even to the point of excitement.

Some people who show or sell halter horses use this to their advantage. The horse is kept locked up in a stable until it is time to be exhibited for the potential buyer or judge – or mare owner if the horse is a stallion standing at stud. Then, when the horse is brought out of the stable, instead of just walking quietly along (which it would if it had just come in from the paddock), it is jumping out of its skin, ready to spook and shy at anything, nostrils dilated, eyes bulging, and tail hoisted high. The horse appears to have great presence and charisma. In reality, sensory deprivation has made the horse bored silly.

Horses out riding can show their intolerance for the same daily routine and their need for excitement. Horses usually enjoy trail riding, but the more the same ride is repeated the less they like it. Some horses show this by becoming depressed and lethargic; whereas others decide to make their own excitement, and start shying at every bird and bush – just for the fun of it. Stallions have an especially low tolerance for boredom, and the best cure is greater variety in work.

Horses are inquisitive and curious, which continually gives them new excitement – as anyone who tries to repair the fence of a horse paddock will find!

Your roll of wire will be worth an exploratory dig, tools become toys to be kicked around and chewed, and your jumper which you foolishly left hanging on the fence is now going to suffer a life-threatening crisis. It is suddenly hoisted into the air by a set of teeth, and becomes so delightfully frightening that the horses snort and leap – and your jumper disappears at a gallop down the paddock. When the excitement is over, your jumper will be stomped to death in the dirt; and the horses will all drift back to see what other amusements you can give them.

This sort of joyous excitement should not be confused with real terror which can be initiated in the same circumstances. A horse may steal your jumper and then become panic-stricken because it is chasing him! The horse will gallop off in terror, not realising that all it has to do is open its jaws to free itself from its tormentor. Such terrors are more likely to affect foals and yearlings because they have been exposed to fewer objects and experiences.

Horses reared in impoverished environments are extremely anxious and fearful towards unusual situations, objects and change.

This excess of fear has been displayed by weanling Thoroughbreds being prepared for public auction. They were stabled indoors without companions or sensory stimulation. Because they were only half the size of a mature Thoroughbred, they were not tall enough to see over their stable doors or internal walls so that when someone opened the stable doors, the weanlings would attempt to climb the walls in sheer terror!

Such horses that are locked up in stables without sensory

stimulation for a long period will become permanently more anxious and fearful. They will also physically deteriorate.

Companions help provide a horse with sensory stimulation; but, as we showed earlier, a companion is not sufficient alone to offset the ill-effects of such mental deprivation.

Additionally, the horse that is reared without the companionship of other horses will fail to learn how to behave with other horses and how to communicate with them.

The communication skills that belong to each species of animals, including people, are not inherent. The development of these skills is dependent on the young animal spending a considerable time in normal relationships with its own kind.[19]

So, a baby that can crawl, and lives in a house full of cats, may imitate the cats and smoodge up against its mother's legs – a form of communication not usual with people! A kitten, deprived of its own mother and reared by people, may fail to learn to purr or miaow. A cow, reared for the first six months of its life in an environment of people and horses, may refuse to have anything to do with cows in its own paddock for all the years that follow.

It becomes obvious that a young animal must be reared with its own species to learn the communication skills of that species. Hence horses must be reared with other horses to learn to communicate with them.

Some researchers showed, with an unkind experiment on monkeys, that in a cooperative electric-shock avoidance learning situation, the isolation-reared monkeys performed poorly in comparison to wild-born monkeys.[20] For the monkeys to successfully avoid receiving electric shocks, they had to be able to communicate with each other and to send and receive information with appropriate facial gestures.

Horses communicate with each other vocally, through

body language, by telepathy, and, to a limited extent, through clairvoyance. The young horse must have the companionship of other horses, besides its mother, to learn these skills. As with people, language can be extremely difficult to learn at an older age.

We've talked of horses being physically and mentally deprived if kept in a small space. However, a horse needs more than the space necessary to exercise both body and mind. It has a psychological need for space. Visual space. Freedom for the eye to cross fences and barriers for mile after mile. Horses love to canter up hills: they want to see what is beyond. Horses paddocked on a hillside will normally spend more time running along the higher boundary than the lower one – they need to get to the top of the hill for visual freedom. It is a difficult thing to explain, for it is a need of the spirit.

Conditioned psychological needs

Horses are likely to acquire extra psychological needs through their association with people. These are needs that they would not develop in the wild state, so they exist only in some horses.

These conditioned psychological needs are usually an extension of a horse's normal essential requirements; and sometimes they are advantageous to us in our relationship with horses, but sometimes they are not.

A horse's natural desire for affection can be extended and enlarged. A horse needs to give affection and to receive affection from its mother or offspring, and its close companions. Thus it can learn to need affection from people too. This can be valuable to us. The desire to gain affection and approval from its owner can be a prime motivator for the horse to try and do what we ask of it. So far, so good.

However, occasionally, very occasionally, a horse will

become so fixated on its owner, so dependent on their approval, that it will be unobliging and uncooperative with other people. In some ways, such horses are like certain breeds of dogs who will only accept one owner in their lifetime.

The need for self-esteem and self-satisfaction is a major one for horses; the horse, like a person, needs to think well of itself. Horses with the highest self-esteem are likely to be found at the top of their pecking order. They are the boss horses: dominant, aggressive, strong-charactered and strong-willed. They are also likely to be the most difficult, independent, bad-tempered, and stubborn; but if they want to work for you they have the strength of character to extend themselves to their utmost limits, and further than other horses.

A horse's need for self-esteem can be extended in different ways to suit us. So the horse may feel the need to excel and beat the others when it is galloping with them, to show the others that it is the dominant horse. Or it may show its need to excel by jumping obstacles better than other horses, or doing the perfect workout in the show ring or dressage arena, producing the most fantastic extended trot when shown in hand, or behaving perfectly with a beginner rider on its back.

This need for self-esteem can be carefully nurtured so that the horse will want to perform to boost its own ego even further. To attain this end, it is important that the horse in training is not out-galloped by the other horses; or out-fenced by too large a jump. The horse has to succeed most of the time to retain its self-esteem and to increase it. Self-esteem is a fragile thing, and if the horse should fail repeatedly, its pride will be broken and its self-confidence gone.

However, with a horse that is naturally high in self-esteem, we will want to make sure that we lead the horse's ego in the right direction, so that it works for us and not against us. A horse that persists in trying to buck us off may have its self-esteem developed in the wrong way!

Needless to say, confrontations with strong-willed horses, or indeed any horse, are usually a battle lost. A horse that has been abused, intimidated, and broken will never have the pride, self-esteem, and affection for its owner which can make a good horse into a great one.

Other conditioned psychological needs can be an extension of a horse's basic requirements, and may be quite destructive to it. So even food and water can become problems.

Horses like eating, and through people they learn a love of eating grain. Most horses who are used to eating grain, if given the opportunity like an open feed room door, will eat too much. The consequences can be fatal!

Even a horse's need for drinking water can become distorted. It quite frequently happens that a horse that has been used to drinking out of a dam or stream, will always refuse water from a trough or bucket, irrespective of how thirsty it may be. The reverse is also true, and the trough-drinking horse may refuse to drink from a dam. This sort of conditioned need makes it very difficult for the horse to be taken out for the day, and makes it completely unsuitable for a day of hard work.

Horses can produce all sorts of conditioned psychological needs, according to how they have been handled by their owners. Some are useful, like the horse wanting our approval; some may be amusing, like the show horse that has learnt the delights of sandwiches and Coca Cola; and some are harmful, or annoying, which include bad behavioural habits. Perverse conditioned psychological needs require some of our best thinking to solve – but then we shouldn't have let them become habits in the first place.

3

THE EMOTIONAL HORSE

To many people the horse's face seems rather unexpressive, and as a result they are unaware of the emotions of the horse.

Horses have many emotions, including such extremes as love and hate, depression and elation, boredom and anger, surprise and fear, as well as many milder emotions in between.

If we understand a horse's emotions we are more likely to succeed in getting it to do what we want, and prevent it doing what we don't want. A calm horse is more likely to be cooperative than an angry or fearful horse. The trouble with extreme emotion is that the horse behaves like us! If we are very angry or excited, we tend not to listen to what other people are saying. So a horse that is overwhelmed with emotion pays little attention to anything else.

It is not only advantageous for us to know which of a horse's emotions are destructive to us having a good working relationship with it; but ideally, if we also consider what the horse enjoys, we can capitalise on it so that the horse will do more for us and give us greater pleasure.

Even so, when handling and riding horses, we really need to be able to *anticipate* their emotions, actions and reactions, rather than simply expecting perfect behaviour and performance from them.

We can anticipate a horse's behaviour and emotions through knowledge, commonsense, empathy, and perception.

We have already considered the horse's needs, which gives us insight as to how it would feel if deprived of them. We can see that a horse's physical needs, like food, will affect not only its health, but also its emotions; and we can see, too, that denial of the horse's psychological needs will only make life more difficult for ourselves. A horse that has had no exercise all day is less likely to stand still for the farrier than one that has just been ridden; and a youngster that has never been ridden out on the road before will be considerably more nervous if it goes alone than it would with a companion.

Commonsense warns us of many pitfalls to avoid in relation to horses. If we pick up the leg of a horse that is not used to it, it may tolerate it for a second or two, and then snatch it back from us. And if we don't let go, it will get annoyed, and swing the leg backwards and forwards trying to wrench it from our grasp. And then it may become very angry, and then few would be strong enough to hang on to that leg! So we avoid confrontations with horses. Instead, we gradually get the horse used to having its feet picked up, little by little, until it will tolerates having its feet picked up for a longer time without causing any fuss. However, if we choose to confront the horse, and to fight it out, the horse will always associate having its feet picked up with anger and fear, and it will always be difficult.

Knowledge and experience are not always enough.

Horses are all different, and will not necessarily behave the same way in identical situations. Even horses that are full brothers or sisters, and have been handled by the same people in the same conditions all their lives, can be very different not only in looks but also in personality.

The ideal situation, of course, would be to be empathic and in rapport with the horse. However, ideal situations are hard to come by, and the next best thing is to be able to perceive a horse's changing emotions – especially if they indicate that we are likely to lose control of the horse in the near future!

There's no way that a farrier can shoe a horse that is so angry or frightened that it is rearing and leaping all over the place. Neither is an overexcited horse likely to win a showjumping contest, because at every jump he is likely to get more and more excited and to concentrate less and less on what he is meant to be doing. We need the horse to listen to us, but we must listen to it, be receptive to it, so that we can anticipate and offset the real possibility of a horse's emotions becoming too extreme and consequently it being most uncooperative.

The differing emotions in horses may be revealed by a slight tightening of a muscle or a movement of the whole body. However, we tend to only notice a horse's emotions when they become excessive, and involve the entire horse. We may see rage in a bucking horse, acute anxiety in a solitary horse galloping up and down a fence, great fear in a horse that cowers and jams its tail down hard between its hind legs, or elation in a pony that has escaped from a yard and is prancing around the paddock in an exuberant high-stepping trot.

On the other hand, we tend not to see the intense depression in a motionless and unresponsive horse, or the annoyance in one that has turned its back on the horse or person offending it, or the anxiety in the tightened abdominal muscles of the showpony expecting the pain of the spur.

We are used to looking at faces, the faces of people, for their emotions and feelings; and when we wonder about the emotions of animals we tend to look at them in the same limited way. Worse than this, we tend not only to limit ourselves to looking at faces, but also to be pre-occupied with whether they smile or not.

The photographer nearly always says, irregardless of how his subjects are feeling: 'Smile! Smile! Say "cheese"!' A smile can charm and delude us so that we accept even lies and insults – providing that they are accompanied by the expected flash of teeth at the same time! In human relations, the importance of the smile makes it the most heartwarming, and the most deceiving gesture of all. We look at the face and, like looking at the Cheshire Cat, we see nothing beyond the smile!

Consequently, many people find the unsmiling face of a horse rather expressionless which encourages them to think that horses are virtually emotionless – that they only have two emotions: ears forward, and the horse is happy; ears back, and he is bad tempered. Even many people who own or work with horses tend to believe this.

An American horse magazine recently published a letter in which the writer complained that every time she visited her stabled horse he greeted her with his ears pointing backwards. So she hit him on the face to make him prick his ears! But to no avail; his ears would only come forward momentarily, and would then return to the backwards position again.

Fortunately for the horse (and even the owner), the editor rightly answered that the horse was just being nice, pleasant, and submissive; and his relaxed ears were showing his non-resistance to her authority.

The owner of the horse had not realised that if the horse was threatening her, that its ears would be *held firmly* backwards, and not just relaxed backwards.

Although horses do have many emotions, the belief in them only having two is also frequently demonstrated by conventional horse photography and in the show ring. The horse must prick its ears so that it looks 'happy': it must not be relaxed and content with its ears backwards, either listening or resting, or else everyone will think that it is 'sour'.

However, horses have a large range of emotions and, from a biological and evolutionary point of view, they have been built in to help horses survive as individuals and as a species. Emotions drive the horse into behaviour which will increase its chances of survival.

Fear makes a horse run from danger; and anger makes the horse, especially the stallion, fight more fiercely those it perceives as its enemies.

Self-esteem or pride gives the horse confidence to try and get what it wants or needs; and success increases the horse's confidence further so it may dare to try and win against greater odds – whether it be stronger horses, an adverse environment, or dominant people. Good racehorse trainers recognise this, and try to avoid their horses being beaten or having confrontations with riders.

However, there is one emotion that is above all the others. Happiness. Like the icing on an emotional cake. Happiness is an emotional response that has become built into us and the horse for doing the right thing biologically.[21] Whatever we do, and whatever the horse does, happiness is the emotional reward for making the correct response to some other emotion.

There is more than relief in outrunning or fighting off danger: there is a real pleasure. 'It was exciting!' we may say in retrospect. And many of us, people and horses, court some danger, to feel the excitement and enjoyment that playing with fear – and surviving – can give.

And with the other emotions, too, happiness follows

doing the right thing biologically. Hence, we not only need to eat and drink, but we also enjoy it; and friendships not only give us the security of being in a group, but also pleasure.

How does happiness affect us and our horses?

If we aim to please our horse, many people would say that we are childish, soppy, and unrealistic, and that the horse should be taught to obey! However, the fact remains that happiness is the dominant need. So, in the right circumstances, happiness can be used to motivate the horse to do what we want; and the horse that does something because it wants to will certainly try harder than one who does something because it is afraid of being hurt if it doesn't. In turn, we will get greater pleasure from the horse.

Which brings us back to the beginning, and the need to recognise a horse's emotions and to respond to them in a way which will not rouse the horse's fear or anger.

The perceptible facial expressions that have been described by other authors are mostly of no real help to us:

(i) Yawning.

(ii) The greeting face: 'happy', with ears pricked.

(iii) The submissive face: made most frequently by foals, and then by yearlings, but only rarely by mature horses. The foal cringes, lowering its shoulders, extending its neck, and raising its muzzle up to the other horse. It pulls up and rounds out the corners of its mouth, and chomps its teeth together rapidly in an obsequious manner, as if it is saying: 'Don't hurt me, I'm only a baby!' A young foal will sometimes make this face to people if it feels uncertain about them.

(iv) The Flehman posture is probably the most curious expression that horses make. The horse puts its head high in the air, muzzle uppermost, and curls back the upper lip

and sniffs long and noisily through its squashed nostrils. Colts and stallions are likely to make this face after smelling urine, but other horses occasionally do it too.
(v) And lastly, the face of rising anger, which should be recognised by everyone.

Although the vast majority of horses tolerate or even like people, occasionally there is one who doesn't. So it is just as well when approaching a strange horse to check that one's presence is, if not welcome, at least accepted.

Horses indicate quite clearly that they do not like someone, or another animal, by narrowing and pulling-up their nostrils so that wrinkles form above them. The ears of an angry horse are also likely to point straight backwards, and are held firmly, unlike when the horse is simply relaxed or even listening to something behind it. Sometimes the horse stretches out its neck at the horse it is trying to warn off and tosses its head up and down at it in a threatening manner. The ears usually only flatten onto the back of the horse's neck when it is all too late, and the horse is already lunging at its opponent with its teeth bared!

We need to be able to perceive more than the five emotions above, and it is easy enough to do so.

As we saw earlier, the extreme emotions of the horse are quite clear as they involve the whole horse; but the same emotions in a more moderate form, or of lesser intensity, like apprehension or annoyance, will reveal themselves differently in different horses; and the horse owner really has to learn them from the movement, gestures, and noises that the horse makes, and the context in which they are made.

So one horse may show apprehension by putting its ears half back at another more dominant horse, or drop its lower eyelids, or extend its top lip, or dilate and round-out its nostrils. Whereas another horse may show annoyance also by putting its ears back, or pawing at the ground, or by grinding its teeth, or swishing its tail, and so on. Many horses may do one thing, but others will do something quite different to express the same emotion.

Consequently, the same gesture in horses may indicate different emotions, and it is the context or situation in which the gesture is used that more fully reveals its meaning. Hence, dilating the nostrils may indicate anxiety, but may also indicate great interest in another horse, or, more simply, the nostrils may be dilated so that the horse can smell and learn something more of its environment.

In the same way, the ears, which we had been led to believe revealed the horse's emotions, are not really good indicators of a horse's feelings on their own. The ears are more like an extension of the eye, pointing where the action is, often flicking forwards, backwards, and even sideways, gathering sounds and information for the horse.

However, in many horses, but not all, the best barometer of its degree of rising emotion is its top lip. We can see the horse's tension visibly increase. Its top lip begins to extend and grow like some sort of elephant-horse, and the corners of its mouth pull up higher and higher so that its mouth looks longer and longer, as if a heavy-handed rider is pulling mercilessly at it. The tendons to the corners of the mouth may stand out clearly like lengths of string, and the facial muscles will become more and more obvious as they tauten and contract in the normal flat plains of the horse's head.

The horse's muscular control over its top lip is very precise, which is why the top lip can do so much and reveal so much: it can function like a thumbless hand, and sort and select preferred plants in the horse's pasture, as well as reveal unrelated emotions with such dissimilar faces as those of anxiety and the Flehman posture.

Some years ago an argument raged in one of the horse magazines, when some Expert declared that many

Arabian horses had a parrot mouth (a congenital deformity where the upper front teeth extend beyond the lower). The Expert stated that the proof of the argument was to be seen in many *photos* of Arabians. She had not realised that some of the horses had been 'jazzed up' and made a bit more fearful or anxious, so that the horse had extended its top lip through tension. This face of anxiety refined and narrowed the horse's muzzle, and so made it more attractive for a photograph!

Horses' emotions can rapidly escalate or change from one to another. An excited horse that is enjoying a gallop one minute, may suddenly become fearful and bolt the next. Or a horse that is peaceable and tolerant at one instant, may suddenly become bored, then resistant, then irritable, then angry and explosive.

One day, some of the grazing horses suddenly saw a small black calf in the neighbouring paddock. They decided that it was very strange and exciting, and a very good reason to gallop around, and to snort and buck, and to carry on like madmen. Then they became bored, and went back to eating the grass. All except one, who had worked herself up into such a frenzy of excitement, that she became quite terrified and galloped straight into a fence – which fortunately was made of pine rails that collapsed harmlessly under the assault.

It is easy enough to recognise the extreme emotions of fear, anger, and elation in a horse, but what about the other emotions? And even more to the point – what are the other emotions?

The English language is particularly rich in words we can use to describe our emotions, which makes it rather difficult to assess how many basic emotions there are. According to the psychologist Robert Plutchik[22] there are eight primary emotions: fear, surprise, sadness, disgust, anger, anticipation, joy, and acceptance. He arranged these emotions on a circle. He equated them to colours, with each one having its opposite, like joy and sadness or acceptance and disgust. Additionally, they could be mixed with their neighbouring emotions so that they formed the secondary emotions of: submission, awe, disappointment, remorse, contempt, aggression, optimism, and love.

People who have spent a lot of time with horses will have seen most of these emotions in horses at one time or another. But, somehow, there seem to be many more emotions than those listed above which are extremely important to us and the horse.

We have already seen how important affection and self-respect are to the horse, and they both touch on Plutchik's basic emotions of love and acceptance.

Horses need affection. Normally the foal receives affection from the very beginning of its life, first from its mother, and then, when it becomes a bit more adventurous and outgoing, from other foals and companions.

In the right circumstances, horses can also learn affection for a person – which not only makes training a horse so much easier, but makes riding and working the horse such a pleasure.

Horses, and people, also have a basic and essential need for self-esteem and self-respect, and they both need acceptance within their group.

The horse that is high in self-esteem is also likely to be high in aggression. It is accustomed to success: success in taking the best food, the most food, the best shelter, the best sleeping spot, and so on. And the more success it has, the more self-esteem it gains, and the more confidence it has to compete against others, or even the environment.

On the other hand, the horse that is low in self-esteem, low in self-respect, will be lacking in confidence and aggression. It will lack an expectation of success when in conflict with other horses, or for that matter people, and will give way to the aggression or assertiveness of other horses. Such horses, whether male or female, will be low in the pecking order, and will be easier for people to manage. In the wild, these lowly horses are the least likely to survive. If they are stallions, they are least likely to find mates and reproduce their less aggressive genes; and if they are mares, due to their lowly position, they and their foals will get least to eat, and they also will be least likely to survive. So we can see how closely connected are self-esteem and aggression in horses.

Sometimes these less aggressive horses can behave very unexpectedly and take us by surprise. We may take a mild-mannered horse, one that is bottom of the pecking order at home, out to ride in the company of others – perhaps at a show or on a trail ride – and find to our embarrassment that it is threatening to kick every horse in sight. Such behaviour is a reaction to fear, of anticipating being hurt by another horse, especially if some other rider comes up from behind. More confident horses tend to ignore the other horses in such situations – unless they are stallions. But there is an exception. A gelding that is accompanied by a mare may be extremely possessive of her in the company of other horses, and may be tempted to attack all and sundry – including other mares!

When we mix up strange horses in this way, it is not surprising that some should display aggression, as the horses have not had the opportunity to work out their social positions in relation to each other.

We mentioned the gelding being possessive of the mare – in fact, being jealous.

Horses can be very jealous, and very possessive. Quite frequently a horse will decide to 'possess' another in the herd – obviously one lower in the pecking order – and drive the other horse around with it all day long. And sometimes horses are very possessive of those who look after them, and may actually be upset, and in rare cases quite distressed, if their owner should feed or touch another horse in their presence.

Hamar was a highly trained imported showhorse, who spent much of his life in unnatural and stressful conditions. As an aged horse he changed hands a number of times. His last owner found he suffered from many anxiety-induced health problems including cribbing, psychosomatic skin conditions, and chronic colic; and also behavioural problems including tongue over the bit, reluctance to eat, fear of being in a large yard or paddock, inability to walk, trot, or canter properly, and sheer terror if he thought he had done something wrong!

However, after a year or so he had recovered from all his problems except cribbing and an occasional bout of colic. He had also developed such affection for his owner, and had become so possessive of her, that if he saw her stroking another horse, he would roar with rage and throw himself sideways against the nearest fence, cutting and scraping his skin so that it bled. Or, as an alternative, he would collapse on the ground – stricken with colic! Naturally, his owner learnt very rapidly never to handle another horse in his presence!

As we have just seen, sometimes horses cannot cope with a situation that causes them great anxiety, and an attack of colic is the result.

The word 'colic' in relation to horses has as ominous a sound as the word 'cancer' does in relation to people. Both are killers. Oddly enough, they are both at times connected to the person or horse suffering from extreme psychological stress or depression from which they can find no relief or escape.

Horses sometimes suffer depression on going to a new

home. They may display their feelings by refusing to eat, and turning a deaf ear to anyone who calls their name. Aged horses, especially stallions, are more like old people, and are more stressed by change than younger horses. And the more valuable the horse is, with the consequent likelihood of it being kept in more confined and stressful conditions – stabled in solitude rather than out in the paddock with companions – the greater the chances of it developing colic.

As we can see, horses have, and even suffer from, many emotions. However, the emotion that is of the greatest importance from our point of view, in its effect on the domestic horse, is that of anxiety.

Anxiety is a debilitating ailment common to both man and beast. It is a state of unease of the mind, and in the horse damages both its health and behaviour.

4

ANXIETY

Most people avoid anxious horses with good reason. We don't normally think of them as being anxious, but simply as being hard to catch, too nervous to ride, or unreliable in competition. Their problems are manifold: besides the obvious troubles of handling and riding such horses, they may also be more difficult to breed or be prone to suffer from minor or even major illnesses.

Anxiety is an emotion similar to fear, but unlike fear, which is a response to some specific danger, such as an attacking stallion, anxiety is a state of *mind* creating a feeling of apprehension that something is wrong without necessarily knowing what it is.

When a horse suffers from chronic anxiety, its body is in a continual state of arousal for physical action with the result that the horse will over-react to any stimuli and it may be constantly jittery and nervous. The horse will misjudge situations, whether they be real or imagined dangers, and be too easily distracted and lacking in concentration to be reliable in competitive or pleasure riding.

Nearly all horses will suffer from some anxiety from time to time, which is perfectly normal, but chronic anxiety is not normal and it is probably the most insidiously destructive emotion possible.

Horses are usually pretty easy going creatures who grow fond of people and attention: why then should some be anxious? The answer is usually found with us.

As we have seen, horses have basic physiological and psychological needs which must be met for them to remain in good health both physically and emotionally. The temporary absence of any of these requirements will upset horses in different ways, resulting in differing degrees of anxiety. However, once the horse's need is satisfied, whatever it may be, the horse's anxiety is alleviated and calm is restored.

In the wild, anxiety serves a useful purpose. The hungry or thirsty horse becomes anxious if it cannot satisfy these needs, and as a consequence drives itself harder to find food or water. Anxiety helps it to survive. However, the horse in captivity usually cannot help itself in anxiety provoking situations: it is dependent upon people for its reduction in anxiety; it relies upon people for its needs. If the need is not satisfied it can have the most injurious results.

The need for food, water, and shelter is clear, but the horse's other needs are less obvious.

Horses need to be able to see different things happening around them, hear different sounds, and smell different smells, and so on: they need variety and stimulation.

Lack of mental or sensory stimulation, in reality enforced boredom, is frequently imposed upon Thoroughbred racehorses, showhorses, and stallions, with devastating results. The anxiety created by the boredom of being locked all night and most of the day in a stable or very small yard with little to look at, forces the horse to create some activity for itself which will help relieve the boredom. Such horses become the weavers, cribbers, and wind-suckers of the equine world.

These forms of repetitive and obsessive behaviour become so ingrained in the horse, that they become part of the horse's ordinary behaviour even when it is not bored. So the weaver rocks from side to side in the float as it is transported down the road, the cribber latches on to a fence post between mouthfuls of food, and the wind-sucker, out in a large paddock with other horses, may prefer to swallow air rather than eat the grass.

People are frequently not aware that horses need companions; and to support this idea they may even point out a horse in a paddock that appears to be grazing alone and away from all the other horses. However, the so-called 'loner' would become very agitated if the other horses were taken to another paddock, and he would try to follow them.

Many horses are kept by themselves, which is stressful for them. Initially, the isolation is likely to make the horse overtly anxious; but as time passes, its restlessness is likely to give way to depression. So if the horse is lucky enough to get a companion at a later date, its owner will be surprised that the horse will appear much happier, and that it will be in better health and condition.

Temporary anxiety has many causes, including depriving a horse of a basic need, disturbing its sense of security, imposing discomfort or boredom, trying to teach it too much at the one time, and fear of pain; but the loss of a companion quite often has catastrophic results.

'Harry' had a paddock full of mares who lived in a semi-wild state, receiving little handling and no extra feed. One day, one of the mares cut her leg, and as it required stitching she was separated from the other horses and shut in a stable without more ado. She was distressed and anxious at being separated from her friends, and rapidly developed colic. Harry was scarcely acquainted with his horse and could offer no reassurance; neither did he think of bringing in a companion horse for the mare. Although she was treated by a vet, it was to no avail. The mare died the following day.

However, most anxiety in horses is related to the fear of pain.

The infliction of pain upon a horse affects it in a very profound way. Due to the process of evolution and survival of the fittest, a good memory and a strong fear for physical danger has been built into horses and reinforced for at least fifty million years. The horse that forgot about the tiger that lived in its lair at the bottom of the hill, or at any time disregarded the danger, would very soon become the tiger's dinner, and so lack the opportunity to pass on to future generations its genes for a poor memory and a low threshold of fear.

So horses normally have good memories and a well-developed instinct for fear. However, their memories do not work in a logical way like ours, but in an emotional fashion and by association. The horse does not remember logically what happened in a certain situation, but it remembers the associated emotion. It does not necessarily remember whether it was hurt or not: it only remembers being afraid.

If we try to shoe or float a horse, and it decides to be uncooperative, and we retaliate with force and anger so that the horse becomes anxious and fearful; the horse will remember that such a situation terrified it. Even if the horse was not hurt, it is part of its biological heritage to remember the fear, and avoid being in that situation again at all costs.

Although some horses will travel in horse trailers as if it

is second nature to them, even without having any previous related experience; and some horses will stand perfectly and quietly for the farrier when they are being shod for the first time; many will not! It is those that will not that need a lot of preliminary experience building up to the Big Event. Otherwise, if the horse becomes too anxious and says 'No!', and we insist 'Yes!', and the horse becomes very upset and leaps and rears all over the place, we have just trained our horse to always become difficult and uncooperative, and possibly downright dangerous, in this situation.

The horse's anxiety has to be kept below boiling point to avoid a continual problem in the same circumstances; and shoeing horses does recur – every six or eight weeks!

Before such Big Events, the horse needs handling to increase its tolerance and confidence for such an occasion.

If the horse is going to be shod, it should already be accustomed to having its feet picked up and filed. If the horse is to be trailered, it should first have some experience of eating its dinner in the trailer. If the horse won't walk into the trailer, it's best to let him eat some of his food standing on the ramp (only of a two-horse trailer and obviously not that of a truck). Then, before he has quite finished, and he's associating the trailer with a good place to be, take the horse away and repeat the Meals on Wheels business again the next day. The next day the horse will be more confident and walk in further. It is a good idea to do this for a few more days before the horse travels.

Occasionally, a horse is completely uncooperative, and won't even put one foot on the ramp – let alone walk inside the horse trailer.

The most important thing is to be very calm – even bored. We don't pressurise the horse so that it gets more and more upset: remember, it will remember! Put a bucket of food on the ramp at a distance from the horse sufficient to make him put one foot on the ramp. We are calm, remember, even bored. No drama, no anxiety. We could brush the horse with a soft brush: it will do both of us good! Keep on brushing. The horse will be confused at first; after all we are behaving rather strangely! But the horse is used to being brushed, or he jolly well should be! He likes it, and he is used to grooming sessions. Perhaps he is used to eating the grass sometimes while we brush him. He's used to being groomed and eating. Now, this is a grooming session: where's the food? Ah! There it is. And one foot thumps on the ramp. Thump! He jumps back, but he already has a mouthful of food. And no one is taking much notice: after all, this is a grooming session, and we are still grooming! So he steps on for another mouthful; and this time doesn't jump back. So we push the food a little higher up the ramp, so he then needs to put two feet on. And so on. If he won't go much higher up the ramp, we tell him how clever he is and take him away. Next day, his confidence should be better, and he will probably progress further.

There are also some other points to consider.

Single horse floats are too claustrophobic for a horse, and there is no room for a companion.

A companion horse who is used to being floated, if floated with the beginner can make the difference between success and disaster.

The large trucks that are used by professional carriers where the horse is sealed up in almost complete darkness and isolation, frighten horses more than two-horse floats pulled by cars or the more open trucks frequently used by professional riders.

A bad driver who drives too fast around corners, or brakes too suddenly will train horses to avoid being floated again!

And what of the horse that is to be shod? Perhaps it is used to us picking out its feet, and filing them, and yet it will not stand still for the farrier. We can see the horse's tension visibly rise. The top lip begins to extend, the corners of the mouth pull up higher and higher, and the muscles in the face take on more and more definition. The horse is going to do a lot worse than just wrench its leg from the farrier's grasp!

We have been talking to the horse, stroking it, and trying to reassure it. We've even growled at the horse, and threatened it with a fate worse than death, but to no avail!

If the horse is thumped by the farrier, or we belt it with a cane, the horse is likely to become so upset that the chances are we will never be able to shoe the horse!

We are going to have to 'bribe' it. Most horses will stand better for the farrier, and be more cooperative, if they are reassured and rewarded. If the handler can manage to hold the horse properly, and feed it lucerne hay at the same time, a successful shoeing is more likely. And because the horse hasn't been upset, it is more likely to be cooperative next time it is to be shod.

Alfalfa is suggested as the reward, as horses like it more than other hay, and it won't matter how much they eat. Whereas there has to be a limit on how much grain is eaten.

There are several other considerations, too, in shoeing horses.

- Horses are usually calmer if shod in familiar surroundings, but it is not fair to use their stable. A horse should be able to feel safe and secure in its own stable: it needs a 'safe-house' where it *knows* no harm will come to it.
- Horses will usually stand better for the farrier if they have been exercised beforehand, and have already satisfied their need for exercise.
- A companion horse nearby will keep the horse calmer than it would be without it.

It may be possible to distract a horse in some other way, than in giving it food, so that it tolerates being shod.

Sometimes it helps if the person who is holding the horse, pats the horse on the neck in exact time to the farrier hammering on its foot – especially if it is the actual hammering that worries the horse the most. So the farrier and the handler both beat the same rhythm at the same time on different parts of the horse.

In summary, if we keep the horse's anxiety down (as well as our own) things will be better next time; and if we let the horse blow its mind with anxiety, or we lose our own temper, no one will even want to try again, and definitely not the horse!

To manage horses successfully, we have to prevent their anxiety rising to the point where they become very angry or afraid. As an absolute last resort, rather than manhandle a horse and make it more fearful, and so teach it to be always difficult in a similar situation, it is better to tranquilise the horse. Then, next time, when the horse is to be shod it will remember not only being shod, but that *it wasn't afraid*. The chances are that we will be able to shoe the horse without any further tranquilisers. However, the use of a tranquiliser is a last resort, and is most unlikely to be necessary for more than one in a hundred horses.

So, sometimes we have to do things with horses that could make them anxious, and we have to work at keeping their anxiety level down.

However, sometimes the situation is quite different and the horse goes out of its way to *make itself* tense and anxious.

Anxiety is the root to many other emotions: a little bit of fear can be called anxiety, an angry confrontation can develop from an anxious niggle, and the need for excitement can develop from the anxiety caused by boredom.

Ginger was bored. He was used to being ridden down the same stretch of road several times a week, and he had seen it all before. He needed some excitement, even if he had to make it himself!

1 Horses need companions. This colt (left) and gelding enjoy being with each other and playing together. The expression on the colt's face says: 'Let's play!' (Chapter 2)

2 Some cats like to be companionable with horses. Even so, horses still need companions of their own species. (Chapter 2)

3 Foals gradually start thinking of greater independence. (Chapter 2)

4 Yawning! (Chapter 3)

5 The Flehman posture. (Chapter 3)

6, **7**, and **8** The author was trying to pose her horse, *Rahalima*, for a photographer, by holding a small dog in her left hand to arouse the horse's interest. (Chapter 3)

6 *Rahalima* shows his jealousy of the dog by ignoring his owner.

7 He remains aloof.

8 When the dog is put down, *Rahalima* responds to his owner and shows his affection.

9 The anxiety of this filly can be seen not only in her wild eye, but also by the extended top lip and the greatly lengthened mouth. (Chapter 4)

10, **11**, and **12** This Arabian colt had to have a series of four antibiotic injections. This is his third injection. The injections were given in a calm and reassuring way so that the horse was not upset, anxious or worried, and so did not behave uncooperatively. No restraint of any sort was used. (Chapter 4)

10 'What was that?' One of the colt's ears has twitched backwards to ask the question. The hypodermic needle has just been placed in his neck and its top is visible in the photo.

11 The handler has connected the syringe to the needle and is pushing in the antibiotic. The colt has lost interest and is looking elsewhere.

12 Reward. The colt and handler enjoy a cuddle.

13 The horse says 'I like you' by mouthing with his lips and tongue the hand of a friend. (Chapter 5)

14 The chestnut gelding is making a submissive face to the stallion and says: 'Don't hurt me, I'm only a baby.' (Chapter 5)

15 The chestnut mare on the right is making the Greeting face and says: 'I like you'. However, the grey mare responds with: 'Fine. But I'm the boss!' (Chapter 5)

16 The handler makes friends with a foal by making herself short and non-threatening, and by gently scratching the foal's chest. The foal's raised foot and extended top lip indicate the foal's response: 'I like you. Play with me!' (Chapter 5)

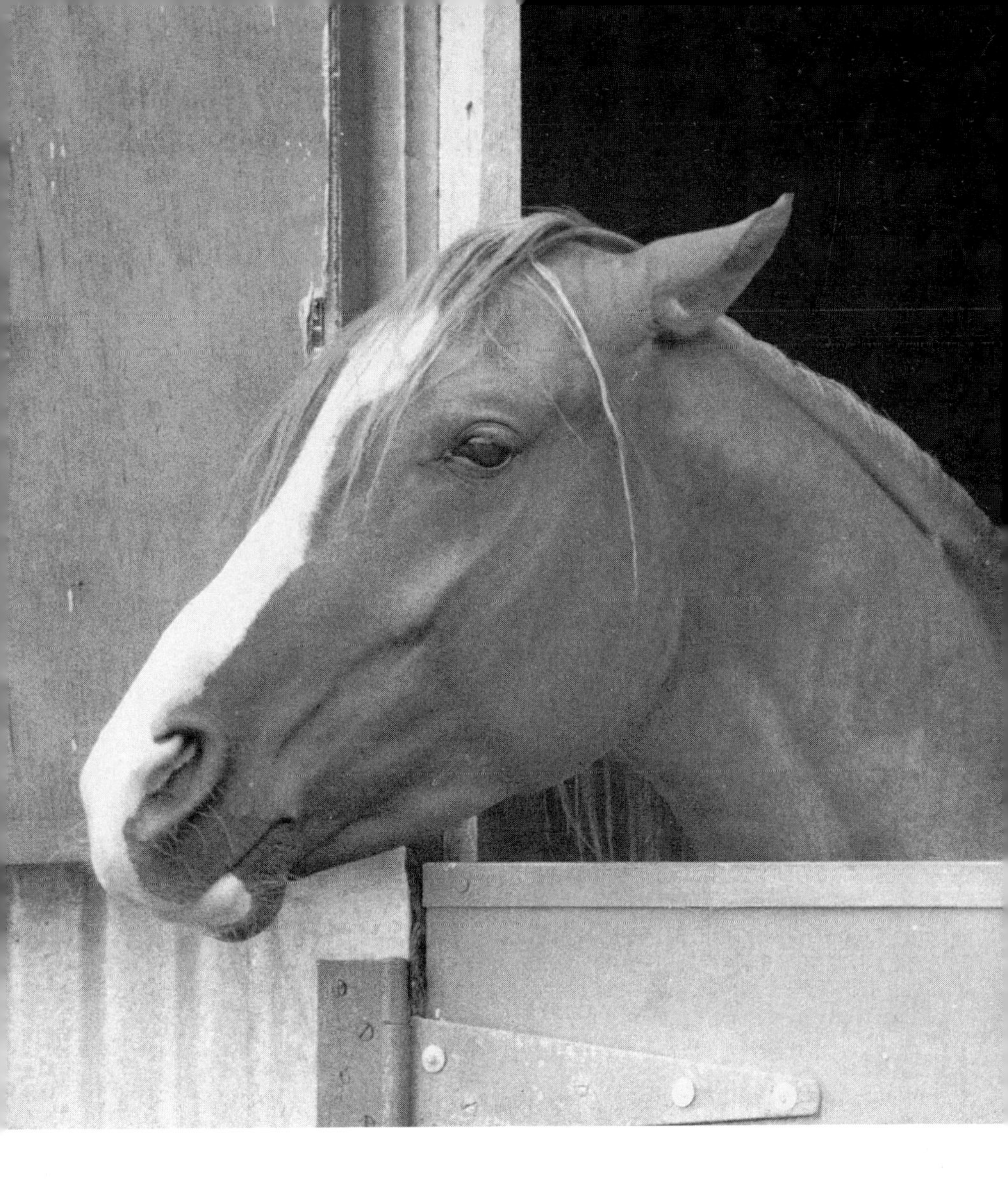

17 This stallion exhibits some aggression in his rather unattractive way of saying: 'I want my dinner!' (Chapter 6)

18 Good natured stallion. (Chapter 6)

19 Unobliging stallion. 'I won't stand for the photographer!' (Chapter 6)

20 This mare is teaching her foal to run away from people. (Chapter 7)

And what was this squatting at the side of the road? It looked like a group of rubbish bins, but they lay on their sides with huge open mouths ready to devour him. How delightfully exciting! And he leapt to the other side of the road pretending to be terribly frightened, to such an extent that he thoroughly convinced himself that he was!

Next day, as Ginger was ridden down the same road, he saw that the bins were still there. So he said to himself: 'This is the place where I was simply terrified!' and remembering his fear of the previous day, he promptly shied again although he had not been hurt the day before.

Irrespective of the cause of anxiety, punishing the horse will only make things worse.

In the wild, a good memory and fear keep the horse alive. In captivity, a good memory and fear will destroy the horse if it is handled so badly that it becomes permanently anxious.

Permanent anxiety is created by the repeated infliction of pain and not by one incident alone. The handler hurts the horse either deliberately or unknowingly: 'Small Brain' may favour an ear twitch; 'Cold Heart' the whip, the ignorant or callous ill-fitting equipment; and 'Hard Hands' the horse's bit; or the horse may have been hurt in some other way.

A horse that has been hurt by people a number of times, especially in the absence of any reward, will learn to expect only ill of people and will always be anxious in relation to them.

Anna was a horse who was born on a stud farm that bred show stock, but unlike her glamorous relatives, she was born ugly. Her Roman nose, and eyes that showed far too much of the whites, continually reminded her owner what a disappointment she was. The other horses were handled and groomed and taken to shows. Anna stayed in the paddock, and her only contact with people was when she was chased into a yard and chute for worming and branding, or else had two legs at a time strapped up to facilitate an occasional trimming of her hooves. A head collar was eventually put on her in the chute, and when she threw her head up in anxiety a roustabout hit her on the face with a lump of wood 'for being so stupid!'

When Anna was three years old it was decided to put her in foal, but many nose twitches, injections, and rectal examinations later, she was still not pregnant; so she was sold.

Her new owner was prepared for some difficulty, and so took Anna to a good professional horsebreaker; but to no avail. After three weeks she was still too nervous to groom, too impossible to bridle. The breaker could make no progress. So Anna was taken to her new home, where she was well cared for, and her new owner tried patiently to handle and groom her. Time passed, and Anna improved a little, but not enough. After two years her owner felt that she had run out of options: Anna was a horse without a future: she could never be a riding horse, nor would she ever breed. No longer are her anxious snorts heard in the still of the night. Too unrewarding and expensive to keep, she was destroyed when only six years old!

Many horses have a lot of negative things happen to them in their lives, like Anna; but unlike with Anna, they are usually interspersed with good things too – which fortunately have an undoing effect. If we do something unpleasant to a horse, like worming it, or giving it an injection, or something else, we are likely to caress or stroke it afterwards, or to reward it in some other way, such as with food. The reward reduces the horse's anxiety and negative feelings, and replaces them with more positive feelings instead – what is often described as 'ending on a good note!'

Not only giving injections, but even branding horses can be done in a calm, easy, and reassuring way so that the horse is not upset. It is not the branding iron or the hypodermic needle that is going to make the most impression on the horse at these times, but our own behaviour, and how we go about it.

If the horse is dealt with brusquely; suddenly brought into a place of noise, shouting people, and strange activity; then restrained and tied so tightly that it is even more anxious; it will be frightened and expect to be hurt, and behave accordingly. It will also have every reason to lose confidence and trust in us, and be more wary of us in the future.

On the other hand, if the horse is brought into familiar surroundings and reassured, the unfamiliar activity necessitated by a branding session involving unknown people and strange activity will not worry the horse so much.

We do *not* tie the horse, blindfold it, or forcefully restrain it in any way.

We simply stand the horse sideways to a solid fence or wall, so that the horse is less likely to think of swivelling around, and stroke its neck and talk quietly to it so that it is relaxed. The brander also walks calmly up to the horse and says 'hullo' and gives it a quiet stroke too. Then, when the brand is hot and the brander comes up to the horse and touches it momentarily on the shoulder (previously clipped), the horse will be surprised, but will probably not even move a step, providing the handler remains relaxed and reassuring.

Other situations can be potentially fearful for a horse. It may be alarmed the first time a bit is put in its mouth, or a saddle is put on its back, or it's girthed up, or mounted, but this anxiety can be 'undone' or prevented altogether by making sure that the horse is not hurt and by rewarding the horse at the same time.

However, if we are unconcerned about the horse becoming anxious, and let it 'buck it out', it may always be anxious in such situations, and it may develop a permanent habit of tongue over the bit, bucking, being girth-shy, or refusing to stand still while it is mounted, and so on.

The destructive effects of anxiety can sometimes be dissipated with reward, undoing the formation of a bad habit, especially if the horse has otherwise been kindly treated.

> Fantasy came back from the horsebreaker with the terrifying habit of standing on her hind legs every time someone got on her back. Fortunately, she was a greedy horse, so when a helper held a bucket of food under her nose for her to eat while she was being mounted, she was easily distracted. Within several days she had forgotten her bad habit and her anxiety, and ceased to require an inducement to let someone climb on her back.

Most horses can be highly motivated to do what we want if we reward them with some favourite food. But there are other rewards, although normally not quite so powerful, such as affection, or caressing or scratching the horse, especially on its chest or neck or some other place that the individual horse may particularly like.

This is not to say we never punish a horse: sometimes we must. If we do, it must be punished immediately, and there must be no doubt in the horse's mind about what it is being punished for.

Occasionally a foal thinks we are pretty low in the pecking order and decides to kick us. Such behaviour warrants a smart kick back on his backside. We cannot afford to ignore such behaviour, because, if we do, the foal will learn to have no respect for us. It will not only knock us around on the slightest whim; but because of its size as a mature horse, it may become dangerous for us and others to handle. However, punishment must be appropriate, immediate, and the reasons for it quite clear to the horse. We also need to reassure the horse shortly afterwards that it has not lost our affection, otherwise it would lose confidence in us.

> Habibi was a really greedy horse! When she was fed 'goodies' on a flat hand, she never left a crumb. One day, her greed was so extreme she bit into the hand itself. The hand promptly slapped her on the neck, and she leapt into the air with shock and surprise; but she was even more surprised when she was offered more feed. Habibi's confidence was restored, yet never was a horse so careful not to bite the hand that fed it! And never again did she make the same mistake.

On the other hand:

> Mary fell off her horse when it bucked. The horse was rather surprised, and stood in the road waiting for her to pick herself up. However, when Mary stood up and took hold of the reins that were trailing on the ground, she thrashed the horse with her cane.
>
> Mary still falls off, but the horse doesn't wait for her any more. She had taught him with the thrashing that he would be punished if he was caught!

The horse may suffer anxiety in relation to one specific part of its life: shoeing, trailering, saddling, mounting, and so on, but if it has been hurt in a number of situations, it is likely to learn to be anxious in relation to anything to do with people. The horse has learnt to associate people with distress or pain, and will suffer chronic anxiety and possibly many problems as a result.

In prehistoric times, if people made the horse feel

anxious or afraid it would run like mad until it had seen the last of them: it fled from the problem, which reduced his fear and anxiety. The modern horse in captivity cannot do this: he remains anxious.

So the anxious horse's body is continually prepared for physical danger, and so for flight – which is a rather inappropriate reaction for ordinary everyday care and riding of the horse. The horse will continually overreact to his handler and everything around him; and he will be nervy, difficult, and 'jumpy' much of the time. He will obviously not want to be caught, and when he is, any number of problems may become apparent.

Anxiety in the horse has many other unfortunate side effects besides the obvious problems of handling and riding such horses. They may be more difficult to breed or suffer from health problems, including major and minor illnesses, such as cribbing, windsucking, poor appetite, skin ailments, and colic.

Anxious horses are more difficult to breed. With stallions, anxiety can turn a normally peaceable horse into an angry, rearing, uncontrollable animal when brought near a mare that is in season. And because of its anxiety, the stallion will try to mount the mare too soon, or from too far away, and may try and attack her or the handler when things go wrong. The stallion's anxiety interferes with its natural instinct: it cannot manage the choreography and mechanics of the situation, its performance is poor, and the mare may not be served properly – or sometimes not at all.

The mare suffers a completely different series of problems in relation to going to stud and getting into foal. In the first place she is anxious because she has been taken from her companions and familiar environment, and placed in a foreign country. What will happen to her? Some mares react badly and their reproductive cycles cease or are disrupted. However, most mares settle down after a few weeks.

Another frequent problem is that brood mares are often brought in from the paddock about a month before the horse is due to foal, and are put in a little paddock next to the owner's house so that 'an eye can be kept on her.' However, she is brought in on her own, and the mare is distraught at being separated from her friends. She aborts, and the foal is lost. (A companion horse should be brought in and kept nearby, but on the other side of the fence – so it doesn't interfere when the foal is born.)

Owners and vets rarely like to consider the possibility of psychosomatic problems with horses, in much the same way as people do not like to admit to suffering from them themselves.

Nevertheless, chronic anxiety in a horse can cause various skin troubles which refuse to clear up with veterinary treatment and antibiotics, but which miraculously disappear when there is a reduction of anxiety.

Sometimes the health problem can be very serious:

> Winsome was a well-bred Thoroughbred brood mare. Some years ago she had gone to stud, with her colt foal at foot, to be served by a stallion who had been very successful on the racetrack. At the end of the stud season Winsome returned home. She was not in foal: and both she and the colt were emaciated, wormy, and covered in lice. Worst of all, Winsome had developed a large malignant tumour on the eyelid of one eye.
>
> Back home she was put in her usual paddock with her old friends, treated for the parasites, and hand fed every day. The tumour could not be treated. However, with restored happiness, improved health, and a dramatic reduction in the horse's anxiety, the potentially fatal tumour regressed and eventually totally disappeared.

Anxiety in the horse, and in people, is cumulative. So the horse may be able to cope with one incident that provokes anxiety and stress; but if two stressful incidents happen at the same time, the horse may be unable to cope and as a consequence refuse to eat or get colic. So a horse may be able to cope with the stress of injury or the stress of being isolated from other horses; but if they both happen at the same time, the resulting stress and anxiety may be more than the horse can manage successfully.

Some horses who suffer chronic anxiety due to poor management or handling, already have a sufficiently high background of stress for only a single stressful incident, like injury, illness, or a new home, to precipitate them into colic or some other illness. Stallions who come from a deprived environment are particularly at risk.

Colic is obviously quite common. What is it exactly? Colic can be described simply as abdominal pain caused by malfunction of the intestinal tract, but sometimes the horse doesn't get better. It has many causes: damage caused by internal parasites, mouldy food or hay, stones and other foreign objects that have been eaten by the horse, or most importantly, stress and anxiety.

It is much easier to see the connection between stress, anxiety and colic, if we remember that problems of the digestive tract caused by stress are also quite common in people. Everyone has heard of stressed executives who suffer peptic ulcers and ulcerative colitis. It is also known that such conditions can be cured by a reduction in anxiety.[23]

As we have seen, anxiety is the cause of many problems in horses. Our only real protection from these problems is for the horse trainer or handler to cure the anxiety before the problems develop – to banish fears in the horse, not to make them.

5

COMMUNICATION

If we know how horses communicate, it not only makes it easier for us to understand them and look after them, but it also makes it possible for us to communicate with them more satisfactorily. Additionally, the greater closeness that better communication brings, the greater pleasure and rewards we will experience with our horses.

One evening Rosslyn's horse came up from the paddock as usual for his dinner, but instead of practically knocking her over like he normally did in his enthusiasm to get at the food, he stopped quietly at her side and put his head in her hands, saying non-verbally: 'I hurt!' Rosslyn realised that the horse was asking for help, and that his manners hadn't just experienced a mysterious and miraculous change for the better during the course of the day! The horse in fact had the beginnings of colic, and Rosslyn's understanding enabled her to help the horse before the situation became too serious. Such understanding can save a horse's life.

A lot of the time it is difficult to know what horses have in mind, and they must find us equally frustrating to understand. The trouble is that people and horses have different ways of communicating, which makes it very difficult for them to understand each other.

Both horses and people will use what they have learnt from their own species and expect the other species to understand. People communicate mainly verbally, and tend to expect horses to understand not only precise commands like 'whoa!' and 'trot!', but also words with a more abstract meaning like 'steady!' and 'easy!'.

People, despite their intelligence, are curiously inadequate at communicating with horses. Most people when confronted with a horse will pat it. Why?

> If two people meet socially, face to face, sooner or later one of them will speak, or acknowledge in some way the presence of the other – even if it's only a nod. Nothing is more uncomfortable to us than a social hiatus, a silence hanging heavily between people in which no one can think of anything to say. We have to communicate: we have a need to be acknowledged by the other.
>
> Perhaps because horses are relatively large, and therefore hard to ignore, people tend to behave in the same way in the presence of a horse.

When we come face to face with a horse we often feel a need or pressure to do something. So we pat it. And patting the horse, even if it completely ignores us, releases our tension. But why pat it? Horses certainly don't instinctively like being patted: a pat is the closest gesture we can make to a kick. Horses like to be caressed, stroked, and scratched; to the extent that they frequently provide this mutual scratching service for each other. So if we wish to touch the horse or communicate with the horse, we should do so in a way that is acceptable to the horse.

People especially like to pat foals, and unfortunately usually on their face or head, which scares the wits out of them. However, by the time a foal has matured, it has usually come to accept that patting is some peculiar human aberration to indicate friendliness – and accepts it as such.

Patting a horse, instead of stroking or scratching it, only has a few valid uses: as a muscular relaxant and distraction; and as a part of 'breaking-in' so that the horse gets used to things thumping around on its back before it is actually ridden.

When a horse is given an injection, it is usual to pat the horse's neck several times on the spot where the needle will be inserted. This prepares the horse's neck muscles so its response to the needle is decreased; and it relaxes the vet's hand and arm muscles so that he or she makes a better job of it!

Additionally, as already mentioned, patting a horse on its neck can be beneficial when trying to shoe a difficult horse; and we pat it in time to the farrier's hammer.

However, patting horses, dogs, or anything else that is large enough, unfortunately seems to have entered into our folklore as being desirable behaviour with an animal.

In the same way, a horse's communication with us will be influenced by the knowledge that it has acquired from other horses; sometimes to its advantage and sometimes not.

If a foal is frightened in the paddock it will rush back to its mother, and seek body contact with her (often at the 'milkbar') for reassurance. In the same way a horse may want to touch a person that it likes. It may want to mouth, not bite, the person's hand; or rest its chin on their shoulder; or brush itself against the person in the same manner as the foal. All of which is behaviour that the perceptive horse owner will accept.

However, sometimes the knowledge that a horse has acquired from its own species brings an unexpected result for the horse when used in relation to us. For example, the horse may generalise from the social structure of its own herd, the pecking order, as a guide of how to relate to us. It may see a man as it would a stallion, and regard him as the Big Boss. It may see a woman as a bossy mare, and best to be avoided. And it may see a child as a foal, and may not find it as intimidating or threatening as a mature person. Hence, the horse may spend the day avoiding mature people, and then find to its surprise that it has been caught by a child-foal that it had not perceived as possessing such ability.

Horses do try to communicate with us, and they expect us to understand. Unfortunately, we expect communication to be verbalised, and preferably in English! So we tend not to understand horses very well. They must get very discouraged.

However, most of us are aware of some of our horse's efforts to communicate, and if we reward these efforts by understanding, the horse will gradually increase its communication with us. We can improve our ability to understand our horse if we can gradually train ourselves to observe it more intently, and to see in what situations and in what context different sounds, movements, and behaviour are used.

How then do horses communicate with each other? The way horses pass messages between themselves will be the way that they will try and impart a message to us.

Horses communicate by sound, sight, smell, body language, touch, and also by extra-sensory perception – the learning of something that has not been transmitted by the other senses. We can include in this category empathy or intuition, and also telepathy.

Most of the time we communicate verbally to each other, and we expect our horses to do the same. However, the number of messages a horse conveys by sound alone is probably relatively limited. Most of us will recognise

'Hullo!', and this may be said so softly that it is almost inaudible and we only see the nostrils tremble. However, if the horse says, 'Hullo, I'm pleased to see you!', the same phrase will be louder and higher. And if we are lucky enough to be very welcome, the pitch and sound will be higher and louder still. We talk in the same way. Our degree of enthusiasm at meeting someone varies from a flat 'hullo', to a higher and more enthusiastic whinny!

In the same way, we may hear the horse's neigh that demands breakfast or dinner, and when dinner hasn't arrived immediately the demand is raised higher and more imperiously, in much the same way as people do.

However, there is one big problem here, and that is that there is not a universal language for horses. Different horses communicate in different ways, although those that live together or are of the same family are more likely to communicate in the same way.

So, if a number of horses ask for dinner, which is a fairly basic demand in horses, some horses may ask verbally but others will summon their slaves by pawing the ground, or banging the gate, or kicking their stable, or tossing their head, and so on.

Another common sentence often called by horses is: 'Where are you?', and the reply of, 'I'm here!', surprisingly sounds just the same! When a horse communicates by sound it is not using language as we would expect it to. In fact, the sound alone does not convey the full idea, but the context in which it is used. This is a very simple form of communication, and one that we use ourselves.

When we go down to the shops we may see an acquaintance on the other side of the road. They see us and shout something we can't quite understand. Perhaps it was 'Hullo! How are you?', but it doesn't really matter. What matters is that we realise that they are being friendly, so we shout back, 'It's a lovely day today, isn't

> it?', or some such thing which they probably will not hear anyway, but the idea of friendliness has been transferred, and both people are happy, although the words were quite unintelligible. So it is with horses.

The sound says I'm sending you an idea. Its intensity usually expresses its importance, and the context in which it is used (commonly in association with body language) gives its meaning.

A horse is put out in the paddock, and failing to see a companion shouts, 'Is anyone there?' The sound itself is the same as when a horse answers, 'Yes, I'm here!', but the sound is also the same as when the horse neighs, 'Hurry up with my dinner!' It is the situation that the horse is in that tells its meaning.

> Sometimes when a person comes home from work and there doesn't seem to be anyone there to greet them, they will call out like the horse in the paddock. It does not matter what words are used (within limits!): it is the calling out that brings the response, not the words. For both the person and the horse, someone will answer if they are there.

Horses can convey considerably more verbal messages than these few examples would imply. A horse uses a number of distinctive sounds to communicate verbally. These vary from the softest gentle breathing-in noise of nostril to nostril getting acquainted, through sniffs, snorts, whinnies, sighs, groans, neighs, squeals, to the ringing roar of a stallion calling a mare, and screams of rage.

These sounds used in different contexts and in different ways and intensity, especially when used with body language, convey quite a large number of different meanings. (We need to bear in mind that the voices of horses differ greatly between individuals; so a mare or foal may actually possess a deep voice, and a stallion may sometimes have quite a high voice.)

Henry Blake[24] states that there are forty-seven basic verbal messages used by horses, although some seventeen of these are used in specific situations like a stallion courting a mare or a mare caring for her foal. Some of these messages are natural to horses in the wild, but some are not. Horses can learn some of the vocabulary of others. So a wild horse will learn to ask for food in the same way as a domestic horse that it may be stabled with, and older foals learn to copy their mothers, and demand their oats with the same imperious neigh.

The body language of horses is the most consistent in meaning, and the easiest for us to understand. Body language is extensive and can be conveyed by the attitude of the whole body or just by a small part of it. We easily recognise the aggressive action of a horse that snakes its head towards a newcomer, puts its ears back, pulls up its nostrils, and raises one leg ready to lash out at the other horse.

We can even see what many horses say to their owners. At a horse show anyone can recognise the horse that is saying, 'You're annoying me!', by the swishing of its tail; or the horse that announces to its spurred rider, 'You're hurting my sides!', by tightened muscles making a clear line along the lower edge of its ribcage; or the halter horse, taut with anxiety and showing the whites of its eyes, telling all but its insensitive handler that it is afraid!

Sometimes body language is not quite so obvious. A horse may indicate that he is annoyed with his owner simply by turning his back on him (like people who dislike each other); or a horse may lick its lips if it is nervous, like an anxious contestant on a television quiz show! A horse standing perfectly in the show ring, with its ears nicely pricked, may indicate that it is cross by pressing its lips tightly together, as if it is refusing some nasty-tasting medicine.

Individual horses will also have their own personal body language. One horse may say, 'I like you', by mouthing his owner's hand with his lips and tongue; another may put his head on his owner's shoulder; or a third may come up to his owner and make some other form of body contact.

It is hard for us to communicate back to a horse with body language, but we can simulate some of the horse's actions.

A horse that is threatening trouble in the paddock we can reprimand with a sharp 'Don't!'; but we can also raise our arm and stab our finger in the air towards it – like a horse with a raised leg threatening to kick.

We know horses like to caress and scratch each other with their muzzles and teeth, and we can copy the same sort of contact on the horse's back, neck, or chest, with our fingertips. Horses also seek body contact for reassurance. If a horse is frightened, particularly a foal, it will rush back to the other horses or its dam for the psychological comfort of contact. So we can calm and comfort a horse in the same way by wrapping our arms around it and holding it closely.

Sight is another form of communication valuable to a horse. The sight of another horse, especially a friend, will calm and reassure a horse that is feeling anxious or frightened. Sight is important to a horse as a passive form of communication; for seeing that all is right in the world around him.

A horse that is returned to the paddock after working may only visually check that its normal companions are there, even if they are some distance away, before starting to eat the grass. Such a horse may appear to be a rather solitary animal, but if the other horses had been removed in his absence, he would have been upset and uninterested in eating. It was sufficient for him to see that all was normal.

Sight is also used in a more direct form of communication. An animal, when threatening to attack another, will stare the intended victim squarely in the eye. This 'eye-balling' by stallions of each other in the show ring is common. Some horse trainers use this knowledge and 'eye-ball' their horses to intimidate them into performing better in halter classes. On a simpler level, we know that it is unwise to turn our back when we are still close to a strange horse, stallion, or foal, because occasionally it will boot us once we take our eyes off it!

Although horses only see in black and white, which is really varying forms of grey like in black and white photographs, they are much more conscious of colour than we would expect. People who give their horses water in plastic garbage bins of different colours, often discover that their horses drink more water from yellow and orange bins than they do from those of a darker colour such as red, brown, green, and purple.

A bad association with a particular colour can disrupt a normally reasonable relationship with a horse.

Jasmine was like many horses: sold as a three-year-old because her owner had found that he could not successfully train her.

Her new owner suspected that there had been difficulties, so decided to start Jasmine's training right from the beginning again. Everything was done calmly and carefully and Jasmine was progressing nicely under saddle – until the day a different coloured saddlecloth was used.

Jasmine's new owner always used white saddlecloths,

> but on this particular day a blue one which was identical in every other respect was used instead. When Jasmine saw that the blue saddlecloth was to be placed on her back, she became panic-stricken, broke free of her moorings, and scattered people and equipment far and wide!
>
> Next day, her owner, in fear and trepidation, tried saddling her up again, but this time with a white saddlecloth. Lo and behold! Jasmine was perfectly serene! Just to make sure that the change in colour of the saddlecloth was what had triggered Jasmine's fear, the blue one was tried again a few days later; but once again Jasmine was afraid. The blue saddlecloth evidently had a strong association with pain; which indicated the reason for her earlier unsuccessful training.

The different colours and patterns of horses' coats also affect their relationships with each other. Horses prefer as companions horses that have the same coat colour as themselves, and tend to avoid those that are radically different. If a skewbald or piebald horse is introduced into a group of other solid coloured or monochromed horses – chestnuts, bays, greys, browns, whites, and blacks – the solid coloured horses are likely to go quite silly, as if they have never seen anything so terrible and exciting in all their lives before! Sometimes competitors in the show ring find that their normally sensible horse has become anxious and irrational; the reason often being because a horse nearby is a flashy appaloosa or tobiano!

We would expect horses to be more comfortable with a horse that looked like itself because it would also be likely to look like its mother. Sometimes when groups of horses get mixed up a foal may seem to get irrationally fixated on another horse. The other horse may even be a young stallion, and be large and overplayful, yet the foal finds it irresistible because it looks like mother!

One of a horse's most important forms of communication is one we rarely consider. It is its sense of smell.

People don't give much value to a sense of smell; unlike the other senses. We measure different degrees in the quality of eyesight and try and correct deficiencies with spectacles. We measure different abilities in hearing and prescribe hearing aids for those that are lacking. But there is no scale for measuring our efficiency to smell. We seem to feel that it is a sense we can manage without. So why worry about a horse's ability to smell?

Horses have a particularly acute ability to smell, and are sensitive to scents and aromas that no person could ever normally detect.

Many horse owners know that their horse can smell *dry* oats or grain, which for us have no odour, from at least several feet away. The grain will be out of sight, and certainly in some unexpected place. The grain may be in a pocket, hidden inside a box, or out of sight above the horse on a bird table. Yet the horse, never having discovered food in such a place before, will stop short in its tracks and say, quite clearly, 'I want it!'

The horse's sense of smell is acute, and it is dependent upon it for adequate communication with other horses. A mare checks her foal by smelling it; and horses check the acceptability of each other by nostril to nostril sniffing; they even check us over too.

When people meet in a social situation, they assess each other visually. They often know from this visual appraisal almost immediately if another person interests them or not. However, the horse usually assesses others through its sense of smell. Its sense of smell must function for it to assess horses it has not met before, and also to fully recognise old companions it may meet in a different environment.

'Lindsay' went to a horse auction. He hoped to buy a young pony that he could break-in and teach his daughter to ride. As the sale was some distance away he took his horse trailer 'just in case . . .'

However, there were no suitable ponies, and indeed the only horses that took his eye in the whole sale were two Arabian stallions. So he hung around the sale to see what would happen to them.

No one seemed to be particularly interested in buying horses of any description – except for the knackers! So when the first stallion, a beautiful bay unbroken three-year-old, was lead into the ring, and Lindsay saw and sensed in the horse many of those virtues that a horse-lover hopes for, he found himself bidding against two knackers, until he had bought the horse for the price of dogs-meat – $185!

The second stallion immediately followed and was an equally attractive horse; chestnut, and full of pride and presence.

'In for a penny, in for a pound!' exclaimed Lindsay with reckless abandon to his wife, who was sitting next to him. 'I'll take him home too!'

So Lindsay had two stallions to take home, and as two stallions are not likely to share the close proximity of a horse trailer without taking each other apart, and probably the horse trailer too, a crowd gathered to watch in expectation!

Lindsay had gone outside with his wife. He stood for a few moments thinking, and looking apprehensively from one stallion to the other. Then turning to his wife, he surprised her with the demand, 'Give me your perfume spray!'

He took the perfume, and sprayed into the nostrils of both stallions. Then, without more ado, he loaded the horses into the trailer.

The horse didn't know if they were Arthur or Martha!

They certainly didn't realise for the length of that trip that they were travelling with another stallion, and the horses arrived at their new home safely.

Lindsay had solved the problem of trailering the stallions together by temporarily wrecking their communication through their sense of smell. Additionally, as the stallions hadn't seen or heard the other *behaving* like a stallion – calling and courting mares, and threatening rivals – they had no particular reason to be suspicious of their travelling companion. Indeed, they were no doubt very glad to have the reassurance of each other's presence for travelling into an unknown future.

We do not have a very good sense of smell, and as a result we are often tactless when handling animals. A jealous horse may resent hands that smell of its rival; a greedy horse may be upset by empty hands that smell of food; and an aggressive stallion may be made dangerous by hands that smell of other stallions or a mare in oestrus.

One also wonders whether it is wise to smoke or to smell of perfume when handling horses.

Some years ago there was a vet, who besides always smelling of methylated spirits, would always conscientiously swab a horse's neck with meths before giving an injection. Then, hey presto! The horse would instantly change from placid and tractable to anxious and difficult!

One day he arrived to give a new-born filly post-foaling antibiotic and tetanus cover. When he walked in the stable door accompanied by his usual aroma, the foal fastened her ears to the back of her neck and attempted to attack him with feet and teeth! The foal is now an eight-year-old mare with a sweet disposition; but then she has never been given a second chance to smell methylated spirits.

> The smell of meths had an unforeseen affect on the foal, and in some strange way stimulated the foal's aggressive instinct.

Horses also use other forms of communication, but they are more difficult for us to understand. They use extra-sensory communication in the forms of empathy, telepathy, and clairvoyance. Actually the word 'use' is too strong. Extra-sensory perception tends just to happen. The most important form is empathy.

A horse that is empathic with another knows how the other feels without it being told through the usual senses of sight, hearing, touch, and smell. So it can receive, or pick up, moods or emotions that convey simple ideas like, 'There's good grass here!' or, 'There's something frightening over there!'

Empathy is a different form of communication from other forms such as verbal, or body language, or smell. It is more passive, less deliberate. In a way it is not a message at all. Just a knowing. Just the general feeling of the horse that is picked up by another empathic horse or person.

Many people are empathic too. At times we may realise that we 'know' something in our mind that has not come about through reasoning. We may be handling a horse and get a feeling that we are in tune with the horse and that it is accepting and even anticipating whatever we want to do: we are in rapport with the horse, and are communicating with the horse but in a way that is not through the other senses.

So, sometimes we get this feeling of empathy and do things with a horse that would not seem to be wise or sensible; but we 'know' that it will be all right, and it is! Conversely, we sometimes do things with a horse that we intellectually reason should be all right, and it isn't!

> 'Elspeth' took her unbroken horse out into an open space. The wind was blowing free, and if there were any

fences they must have been beyond the distant horizon. The horse hadn't been mounted before, and it wasn't restrained – beyond wearing a bridle and saddle. Neither was it hobbled or tied. No one else was there. Yet Elspeth 'knew' that it would be all right to mount the horse, and it was.

Next day Elspeth went to mount the horse again, but this time she was chatting to a friend instead of listening to the horse. She had reasoned that as she had already mounted the horse and walked around on it the previous day, that this time it would be easy. She never managed to remember how she landed on her head instead!

We seem to be able to communicate better with a horse if no one else is around. If we are just with the horse in an easy fashion, empathy comes more easily.

Henry Blake experimentally proved the existence of empathy between horses through using pairs of closely bonded horses who were mentally and emotionally close to each other; and he discovered that horses could communicate with some horses through empathy, but not with others.

Horses of the same family or the same breed are more likely to be empathic, and so to get on together the best. Thus Thoroughbreds, Arabians, Shetlands, and so on, will prefer as a companion a member of their own breed. Dissimilar horses, like a Shetland and a Thoroughbred, may have a lot of trouble relating to each other, and maybe never will. However, over a long period of time and association, horses and ponies can alter their thought patterns and learn to think more like each other, and to become more empathic. Eventually they may grow to like each other, especially if there is some other link they can make with each other such as matching colour.

Horses are also telepathic. Telepathy is like empathy, except the message is less generalised and more specific.

> 'Jenny' was eating dinner, and enjoying it. Then it came to her that something was wrong with her horse. She *knew* something was the matter. The steak was left to congeal on the plate, and Jenny ran down to the stable as fast as she could. And there was the horse, lying on the ground, cast against the stable wall.

Henry Blake experimented with telepathy between himself and horses. He found that he could direct a free horse to choose the correct feed bucket – the one containing oats whilst the others were empty – by visualising in his own mind the oats lying in the bottom of the bucket. However, he had to have a close feeling of empathy with the horse in the first place to be able to transmit the mental idea. So, only some horses were receptive to such telepathic messages.

The visualising of objects can sometimes help when we are out riding. If we see something on the side of the road, and we think the horse may shy at it, and we look at it very hard and carefully, the horse tends to be less likely to shy.

Feeling something very strongly in our mind often becomes communicable to the horse. We may simply be afraid, and the horse picks it up too. Or we may be determined to catch a horse that doesn't want to be caught; and if we feel it strongly enough, the horse seems to feel our determination too, and suddenly stops running away from us and agrees to being haltered.

Telepathy often seems to happen between horses and people in more dramatic situations.

> Gidget was a part-Arabian horse, and she was empathic not only with her special equine friend Tang, but also with her owner 'Karen'.
>
> One day Tang was stolen. Karen reported the theft to the police and the ranger, and spent hours driving

around the roads looking for Tang. But to no avail.

Several days later Karen noticed Gidget just standing, staring across the paddocks into the distance. Intuitively, Karen decided to go where Gidget appeared to be pointing, although it meant crossing very difficult country. She walked in a straight line. Across peoples' properties. Through fences and barb-wire, over the top of a rocky hill, and down into a hidden valley. And there, behind a house, was Tang!

According to Henry Blake, horses also use clairvoyance – the transmitting of a mental picture. He says they do this 'to direct other horses to food and water, especially over distances where they were out of earshot and out of sight of each other; or to split the herd in time of danger'.[25] In a period of ten years he recorded at least thirty proven cases of clairvoyance between himself, or his wife, and a horse. Three of these occurrences were across distances of over eighteen miles.

Thus, there are many forms of communication that horses use, from body language to empathy. Nevertheless, they are rarely used individually and to the exclusion of all other forms of communication, so they need to be considered all together; each form of communication adding a little more to the message the horse is sending.

However, this is all rather analytical and intellectual; and if we ourselves can only function on this rational level, our communication with horses will be no better than a tourist who needs a phrase book or dictionary in a foreign country. From our point of view, empathy is the most valuable form of communication with the horse, for we not only have insight into how the horse feels, but we intuitively understand the horse's other forms of communication, like verbal messages and body language.

6

TEMPERAMENT AND INTELLIGENCE

Temperament

We don't talk about the character or personality of horses very much, instead we talk about their temperament.

We are used to everyone saying that their horse has a good temperament, but what is the temperament of a horse? Everybody seems to say something different. The owner of a competitive jumping horse says that his horse has a good temperament because it is 'consistent and courageous'. The show exhibitor's horse 'has presence and a smart way of going'; the pony clubber's horse may be 'willing and lovable'; whereas the horse dealer's horse has every virtue that anyone has ever heard of: 'What ya want, she's got!'

From these answers we can see that a horse's temperament may touch on all these statements, or their opposites, and that the horse's temperament is demonstrated by its general or most consistent mood and natural disposition. (If the horse is inconsistent in its moods we call it temperamental!)

The horse's temperament is the inherited part of its personality. It will consist of a number of relatively enduring traits, or ways in which one individual differs from another, and it will be the foundation on which the horse's personality is built. The horse's temperament, along with the effects of its environment, learning, and handling by people, will determine the horse's mature personality for better or for worse.

The horse's temperament is extremely important to us, because as its basis of personality it will interact with our personality and determine how successful our horse-partnership will be.

Psychologists have never had much success at defining which personality characteristics are inherited in humans and which are not. They have argued for decades as to whether we are a result of our environment or our genetic inheritance, and there are always supporters for each extreme as well as for every position in between.

One of the problems in deciding how much of a person's temperament is inherited is due to the fact that babies are usually brought up in an environment of both parents, or at least more than one individual, and that they take a while to grow and show many personality characteristics. Consequently, it is not easy to perceive what characteristics are inherited from a particular parent and which characteristics are copied or learnt.

However, with horses the situation is quite different. Foals are considerably more active and responsive than babies. Additionally, the father of a foal normally has no contact with it. So if a foal exhibits characteristics or mannerisms that are not displayed by its mother, or other horses that it is with, but only by its father, such a characteristic would appear to be inherited. This would seem to be especially true when the foal exhibits a characteristic that is clearly opposite to how the dam herself has behaved from the time of her birth.

> 'Pete' was an old horseman. In all his sixty years he had bought, sold, bred, and trained some hundreds of horses. He had seen the best and the worst. In fact he still had the worst – a mare called 'Bint Pomona.' She was the result of unwittingly having bred together two horses of exceptionally unobliging, unwilling, untrainable, and stubborn temperament; to produce 'the worst horse in the world' thought Pete ruefully. And there was no way in which Bint Pomona could be induced, cajoled, enticed, bribed, threatened, or made to oblige people in any way. 'I can do it', she would say when people tried. 'But see if you can make me!'
>
> So, Bint Pomona became a brood mare (which was also a mistake, because her foals all had the same temperament as her). She continued being 'the worst horse in the world' until one year she was served by yet another stallion; but this time the stallion worked a genetic miracle upon the foal which was quite happy to be taught anything!
>
> From then on, Bint Pomona changed, at least in Pete's eyes, from being 'the worst horse in the world' to 'one of the best' – because (with help from the stallion) each year's foal was now as good as gold!

The next problem of course is how many different characteristics or traits of temperament are inherited? These characteristics must be quite separate, and not dependent on or part of something else.

The enormity of such a task has been made obvious by an American psychologist in the 1930s, who worked his way through an unabridged dictionary, and found that there were about eighteen thousand words that could be used to describe people.[26] Although a list of words describing horses would be shorter (we could leave out words like idealistic or religious), we are still left with a vast number. Fortunately, however, most of them are closely related to others, and the separate characteristics which concern us are relatively few in number.

These characteristics, which are inheritable, concern us because they are going to have a profound effect on our relationship with the horse. They will determine whether a horse is willing or uncooperative; docile or aggressive; confident or anxious; sensible or unpredictable; trustworthy or mean; friendly or standoffish; tolerant or impatient; and animated or placid.

These characteristics are not linked. One might expect a docile or sensible horse, or even a friendly one, to be willing. Don't believe it! This is only true sometimes. Or one might expect an aggressive horse to be mean and uncooperative, but this is not necessarily true either.

'Inanna' was such a beautiful horse that she was named after the Sumerian Queen of Heaven. However, the Sumerian Queen was a tough lady, and always got her own way, and Inanna did too.

Inanna had been bred by her owner and loved people. She would even leave the company of the other horses and follow her owner around the paddock in the hope of a cuddle. So it was a great disappointment to discover that she was quite unlike all the other home-bred horses, and that she would give nothing in return to those who cared for her and bestowed affection upon her.

Inanna had inherited from her mother a particular form of behaviour to use when she was anxious or didn't want to do something. She ran backwards. While she had inherited from her father, and the stallion's father before him, a stubborn and cussed temperament.

> So, if she didn't want to go anywhere, and she frequently didn't, she ran backwards; even if it was straight into a prickly bush or a stinging cane. Much of the time she could only be ridden towards her dinner bucket; any other direction except backwards produced complete refusal. She was even deliberately ridden backwards, which is very hard on a horse, to make her want to go forwards for relief, but she still refused to move on. And to cap it all off, when she was tied-up she couldn't run backwards, so she lay down instead!
>
> Inanna was the most beautiful, friendly, and uncooperative horse that one could ever have the misfortune to own; because from her looks she promised so much, but from her heart she gave so little!

A horse's degree of willingness, cooperation in learning new things, agreeableness in doing what we ask of it, are most important traits in a horse's temperament if we wish to enjoy riding it; yet it is an aspect of the horse that is more overlooked than any other when someone is thinking of buying or breeding a horse. The trait of genuine willingness in horses is not as common as horse lovers, breeders and dealers would have us suppose.

Horsebreakers and trainers sometimes equate willingness with lack of intelligence, and intelligence with a lack of cooperation. 'The horse is too clever for its own good!' is a frequent complaint when a horse evades or refuses to do what is expected of it. However, willingness and intelligence are two quite separate traits in the horse.

Willingness is a highly inheritable trait, and its presence can be seen quite clearly in the off-spring of some stallions who have an exceptionally willing temperament. Its complete opposite, stubborness, obstinacy, refusal to cooperate, 'I know how to do it, but I won't!' can also be seen in entire families of different breeding.

Willingness is essential for a good child's pony, and one

would think necessary, although perhaps to a lesser degree, for most adults to really enjoy riding too. Nevertheless, there are always some cowboys who like to argue with all and sundry, including their horse.

Aggression in a horse is an aspect of its personality which continually concerns us. As we have said before; horses high in aggression are more likely to have been the survivors during the processes of evolution. So aggression is very much part of the horse's biological heritage.

From our point of view, this doesn't sound too good. Who wants an aggressive horse?

However, aggression in the horse does not mean that he will be aggressive or hostile towards *us*. And because aggression is not related to other traits of personality like being cooperative, friendly, or trustworthy; the horse may be a paragon of virtue to ride. Additionally, an aggressive horse has the courage and determination to be a top performance horse, if he also has the physical capabilities and the motivation.

Aggression in a horse is displayed in different ways. In a few cases people are the target, usually the result of the horses not having being handled properly; but mostly the aggression in horses is directed towards other horses. It can also be minimal or extreme. So there are many different situations that involve aggression that will call for us to respond in different ways.

Minimal displays of aggression towards us are usually best ignored. Even the most mild-mannered and good-natured mare is likely to approach her dinner bucket with her ears flat on her head, but as soon as she has buried her nose in the oats, she relaxes. A stallion that behaves in the same way is psychologically more threatening to us, but it is best to respond with tact – to stroke the horse briefly and then to leave it in peace. Many horses prefer to eat by themselves, which is a basic response to a fear of losing their food.

Of course if a number of horses are being fed in a paddock, their feedbins should be spaced well apart and there should be one for every horse. The horses should be fed in descending pecking order, starting from the herd leader, otherwise fights will result.

Normally, if a horse acts aggressively towards us we let it know quite clearly that such behaviour is unacceptable, and punish it appropriately and immediately, so that there is no doubt in the horse's mind what the punishment is for.

So, if we are grooming a horse and it tries to cow-kick us, we retaliate with a sharp verbal reproach or a smack with the flat of the hand, and usually the horse decides to accept that we are the boss and minds its manners in the future.

However, more aggressive horses, especially colts and stallions, will be more likely to respond to our aggression with aggression, which we should expect. It is their instinct to do so. So a stallion may respond to punishment from us by trying to kick us with greater determination instead. To respond to this situation with further physical punishment is to invite war; one which will greatly damage the relationship between horse and person.

There are a number of ways around such a situation. For example, if the horse kicks when we are trying to brush its legs, we don't swat it with the cane. Instead, we keep calm and persevere. We go on brushing. However, we don't want the horse to get really angry, and to associate having its legs brushed with anger and a need to kick. So, on the first day of brushing we just brush as much as the horse will tolerate. Then, next day we brush a little more. And gradually we brush a little more each day and try to gradually increase the horse's tolerance, until we can brush the horse all over without any trouble.

Secondly, if a horse is aggressive towards us, it is better to try and get the horse to accept the fact that we are the boss horse, not by punishing it, but by teaching it something. So the horse gets used to doing what we want by suggestion rather than by domineering authority and punishment, and continues to do what we want through respect, habit, and a growing trust and affection for us.

Horses that are well handled from the time of being foals are most unlikely to be aggressive towards us. The young horse goes through so many learning experiences with us – the discipline of being held still in our arms as a foal, acceptance of being stroked all over and having its legs picked up, learning to lead and to be tied up, and later learning to accept being rugged and lunged. If we do it correctly, the horse learns not only to be confident with us and to respect us but also to like us. Confrontations are quite unnecessary.

Teaching the horse to respect us, by teaching it something new – leading, lunging, and riding it – is the most effective way of dealing with aggression in the younger horse. Old aggressive horses are another problem altogether. Someone has already taught it to be aggressive towards people: they have reinforced a natural tendency for aggression and its expression. And bad habits are very hard to undo. The horse's behaviour may be modified by trying to get it to have confidence in us and to like us; and by keeping our own aggression under control, so that we don't arouse the horse's aggressive instinct. Most importantly, we need to avoid situations where the horse is likely to express its aggression towards us, at least until the horse has learnt to respect and like us to some extent.

Moz was an Arabian stallion bought at auction. His early history was not revealed, but when he arrived at his new home he was hostile, aggressive, and even savage; and people were forced to take to their own heels to save themselves from his!

No one could go into his yard without a cane – which

he appeared to be terrified of – and the viciousness he displayed when anyone was near his food was so extreme that the only way he could be fed was to throw his food over the fence!

'It's tough on a horse going to a new home, especially a stallion', his new owner said. 'He will settle down.' But he didn't. His hostility was unabated.

Moz was almost impossible to handle. If someone carried a cane he was so scared he couldn't be caught; and if the person didn't carry a cane Moz tried to attack them!

The problem was eventually reduced by putting a headstall on him with a long rope attached. Then, when his owner wanted to catch him she would grab the rope which was trailing on the ground, and take possession of his head before he managed to rear up on her or kick her with his hind legs.

She then tied him up.

Moz's dinner could then be brought into the yard without dumping it over the fence; and the horse was then led up to this food, caressed a few times, and released while he was still distracted by eating the first few mouthfuls. His owner immediately backed out of harm's way.

After a few days of this treatment, Moz began to feel less threatened by his owner, and began to greet her at the gate. So now he could be caught behind the safety of the fence, and the rope attached to his headstall was no longer needed.

So things improved; although he still tried to bite, kick, rear on top of people, run them down, or crush them into fences, if given the chance. The key to managing him was in keeping calm, and avoiding situations where one could be trapped and hurt. And if one had to put oneself in a vulnerable situation, like

> rugging or grooming him, the handler had to carry a cane.
>
> After six weeks Moz began to mellow, and the headstall no longer had to be kept on him. It could be put on and off each day, although with difficulty. Fortunately, he was a clever horse and learnt easily. So he learnt that if he gave a little he could expect a reward. If he allowed the headstall to be put on him, he was rewarded by being put out in the paddock, or brought in for his dinner, or taken for a ride. Life improved. Whereas, if he leapt around, stood on his hind legs, and tried to eat a pound or two of human flesh, the headstall was not put on him and he wasn't taken anywhere.
>
> After another six weeks, the cane, which never once had been used, was put away permanently. Moz had become a reformed character. He still made some shows of aggression, but more as a dangerous game than with wicked intent. And it continued to prove tactful and wise to respond to such displays with great calm and care.

We've already talked of anxious horses, and how no one would have one for preference. Some horses are actually born more anxious than others, and it makes them particularly difficult to train. Such overly anxious and insecure horses are usually found amongst the Thoroughbred population, where speed is of such importance that it predominates over every other desirable characteristic. Fortunately most horses aren't born anxious, and it is natural for young horses that are well handled to be confident and friendly.

Some horses are born sensible; others definitely are not, and may be silly, unpredictable, and unreliable. If a horse is sensible it does not mean that it is plain and ordinary – like an old pair of shoes – rather, being sensible is exactly that. The horse's reactions to its environment are more likely to be consistent, reasonable, judicious, moderate, and practical. Fortunately, sensible horses are found amongst all breeds.

When we consider temperament in horses, and especially in families, it is most reasonable to look at the stallions in a family to get a more valid picture of the family characteristics, as stallions often exhibit traits of temperament to greater extremes than geldings and mares. This is especially true of the very different but forceful characteristics like aggression and meaness. It sometimes happens that yearling or two-year-old colts show signs of aggression, and treat people like an inferior horse. Many of these colts are castrated, and as geldings they become more docile and respectful. So, if a stallion should exhibit a particularly kind and mild nature, it would indicate that the stallion's family could be kinder and more trustworthy than other horses in general.

Aggression and meaness are completely different characteristics. Aggression is related to anger and hostility; whereas meaness relates to spitefulness and untrustworthiness. Many horses are aggressive, but fortunately few are mean, and those that are have most frequently been made that way by people.

However, meaness and untrustworthiness are not the perogative of stallions alone, and some of the meanest horses are mares, and even children's ponies!

'Hi Jinks' appeared to be perfect. All eleven hands of her were so pretty, and so faultless, that whoever saw her always wanted to take her home. And take her home they did – never understanding why the previous owner had been so happy to part with her!

They usually found out fast enough. Hi Jinks had an awesome range of martial skills which she practiced on small children. She not only bit, kicked, and knocked them down; but she would also hold a child on the ground by wrapping her jaws around the child's throat, or bite a child in the face.

It's extraordinary how mean some horses can be. It is also equally extraordinary how mean some people can be to pass on such a pony to an unsuspecting family with small children!

However, in all fairness to such horses and ponies, many are made mean by callous adults. It seems some parents let their children amuse themselves by chasing foals and small ponies, or throwing sticks and stones at them, or tormenting them in other ways.

We like our horses to be friendly, and usually they are born friendly, but whether they are to remain friendly is determined very much by our handling of them.

For the first three days after a foal is born it is usually fairly accepting of the world around it, and it is of considerable advantage to us to make use of these three days to teach the foal that we are friendly and trustworthy. We caress the foal and it learns affection for us. We hold it in our arms, and it learns not only discipline and respect for us but also reassurance and security from our close body contact. We stroke it all over, from its tummy to its toes, and it learns to accept us, and is not frightened or afraid. However, if we neglect to make use of these first three days of a foal's life in this way, we are likely to find that the foal becomes suspicious of us. It will run away from us. It will be difficult to catch; and if we do catch it, we may not be strong enough to hold it. And if we can hold it, the foal will still be frightened of us, and we will have to give it a lot more handling than we would have had to do initially to undo its instinctive fear of us and learn to accept us instead.

So how we handle the foal is certainly going to make a difference between whether the mature horse will be friendly or not, and in my experience, horses that have not been well handled as foals are never as friendly, trusting, and confident as those who have. It is for this reason that the horse reared for the market-place seldom has the charm, intelligence, and friendliness of the horses bred for personal pleasure.

However, some horses are not born friendly, and even if many long hours are spent handling the foal, it may never be really friendly, and in fact may be rather stand-offish. Nevertheless, it will be a much easier horse to handle, for example to catch, than if it had not had this early contact with people. So some horses are unfriendly because it is part of their genetic makeup, and other horses are unfriendly due to lack of proper handling when they are young.

However, whether a horse is friendly or not has no bearing on whether a horse is a good riding horse: some horses who are very good to ride show no indication of liking people at all. Friendliness is not a necessary attribute in a horse; it is just a pleasant one.

A horse's degree of tolerance, or passivity, as opposed to impatience and irritability, will be very important in relation to what we want to do with the horse.

The Egyptians have always favoured the Arabian horse. However, in spite of having continually plundered Arabia through the centuries and taken thousands of its best horses, by the beginning of this century few of their descendants remained and those that did were in a very sorry state of deterioration.

In 1908, the Royal Agricultural Society of Egypt realised that the Egyptian horses were 'showing some signs of deterioration'.[27] They decided to upgrade their horses by using foreign stallions, but as they were unable to buy Arabian stallions they decided to use English Thoroughbreds instead.

However, the Egyptians were bad and cruel horse-keepers. 'The native habit of tethering horses and hobbling them in the full glare of a torrid sun (with a temperature of perhaps 120°F. in the shade) destroys the strongest constitution and often kills them outright . . . Closely hobbled with tightly drawn ropes they can only move by laborious hopping with arched backs . . . Half starved and half blinded with glare and flies they are in a sorry condition of thirst and misery. Yet no one gives two thoughts to their condition. It is the custom of the country'.[28]

The Royal Agricultural Society of Egypt continued using English Thoroughbred stallions until 1914. But, according to the Egyptians, 'the experiment of crossing English horses with Arab mares was unsuccessful, for the offspring proved both vicious and ugly, and were very unpopular . . .'[29]

Really!

The Thoroughbreds were replaced by Arabians – many of which were imported from England.

In short, the Arabian horses had greater tolerance than the Thoroughbred horses.

Although we are not going to be hobbling a horse by three legs and tethering it all day out in the sun, we will need a tolerant horse if we wish it to do boring or repetitious work. So we will need a tolerant and patient horse if we want to use it as a school horse, or a plough horse, or even a dressage horse.

If we push the horse beyond its limits of tolerance, we will find we have made our horse anxious, sour, angry, or even vicious – like the Thoroughbreds and Anglo-Arabian horses in Egypt eighty years ago.

A horse that lacks tolerance and patience will seem impatient and even irritable. It will be keen to get going. It won't want to stand around while we talk; and if we get off its back and tie it to a fence, it will dig a hole in the ground through sheer impatience.

Such horses are hopeless at dressage, because they always decide what we should do before we ask them. So they anticipate the markers, and change pace before we reach them. However, in unstructured riding, like hacking; or in a situation where the horse's instinct is valued, like with a stock or cow horse, its anticipation of the rider's wants is a great asset.

However, it is easy to confuse intolerance with anxiety or lack of cooperation. Nevertheless, all three can be quite separate and distinct parts of a horse's temperament.

An even less easily defined aspect of a horse's temperament than tolerance, is the horse's cheerfulness, gaiety, animation, or 'smart way of going'; with its opposite being placidity and peacefulness.

Placid and peaceful ponies are usually what people want for their children, and with good reason. They are often advertised in the newspapers as 'bomb proof!': no matter what occurs they will just continue their mild sweet way as if nothing had ever happened.

However, for show purposes and parades, people like a horse that says 'look at me', and to have this presence they need not only good looks but also some essence of animation or cheerfulness.

We expect all horses that are well looked after to be cheerful, but like people, some display it more than others.

Most foals are playful, but like other animals and even ourselves, as they mature and the years go by this characteristic diminishes. With some horses, animation that is not a response to anxiety or fear, becomes a thing of the past; but with others, especially Arabians, cheerfulness and animation continue as a consistent part of their personality. This may be seen in a certain gaiety under saddle, or a continual alertness that isn't anxiety, or in exuberant air-borne paces with tail hoisted high.

And what about humour? Many people swear that their horse has a sense of humour, especially when it likes tipping them off; but it is possible of course that these people actually have a considerable sense of humour themselves to put up with the vagaries of their horse!

Jester was an appaloosa stallion who had a very close relationship with his owner. Together they worked hard on a sheep station. It was hot, dusty work checking endless fencing and huge flocks of sheep; so every now and then they stopped at a trough at one of the wells, so that Jester could drink and his owner could splash his face and arms in the water.

One day, Jester had finished drinking and he was watching his master with a languid eye. The man was bending over the trough, sloshing handfuls of water everywhere. Jester let his head sag lower and lower as if he were falling asleep. Then suddenly he thrust his head between his owner's legs and hoisted him into the trough with a resounding splash!

If horses have a sense of humour, it is of the slapstick variety. It depends upon the incongruous, perceiving what is out of place – which is usually us! It seems to be shown in situations where we have been disadvantaged. We laugh at the absurd and ridiculous; perhaps horses do too.

Beauty was a draught horse who belonged to a suburban dairy. She had a special driver, who unlike some, cared for his horse and never overworked her. And Beauty in her turn was sober, sensible, and one hundred per cent reliable – until the day she carefully picked up in her teeth a full bucket of water, and then just as carefully poured it over her owner's head!

Some horses also like to tease us, to irritate us with trivial annoyances – and especially in front of an audience.

Hazar, an Arabian stallion, felt that halter classes at shows were rather beneath his dignity. He liked to reverse the situation of being led around the ring, by grabbing with his teeth his owner's arm by the cuff of her coat, and leading her around the ring instead. And there was no way he could be prevailed upon to release it without an embarrassing fracas in front of the judge!

Intelligence

Although intelligence in a horse, or lack of it, is also an inherited characteristic, it is not part of a horse's temperament. However, it also affects how one individual interacts with others and so is often confused with aspects of a horse's temperament. For example, a horse that will not do something we may call 'stubborn' or 'pig-headed', when in fact it does not know what we want. Or another horse may be described as 'too intelligent for its own good!' when in fact the horse is actually demonstrating an unwilling aspect of its temperament when it evades what is being asked of it.

When we talk about intelligence in horses, we are usually referring to how quickly they learn something. Horses have a very good memory, and an intelligent horse may learn something from a single incident. A less intelligent horse may need a repeat occurrence or lesson several times before it remembers in the future. But this all gets mixed up with motivation too: the horse must be motivated to learn.

Although horses have a very good memory, they have a

poor ability to reason. If we teach a horse to move to the right away from the pressure of a rider's leg on their left side; they do not seem to be able to reason that pressure on the right side is intended to make them move to the left. So, whatever we do in training the horse, we have to teach on both sides: what it learns for one side, it will not automatically accept for the other.

Although intelligence in the horse is an inherited characteristic, our handling of the horse will affect it as much as handling affects different characteristics of temperament.

We would expect handling a horse when it is young to affect its friendliness towards people, but we would not necessarily expect handling a horse when it is young to affect its intelligence. However, this does appear to be the case.

When we handle a young horse correctly, we not only caress it, hold it, and stroke it, and pick up its feet; but we teach it to lead. And to lead the horse we need to go somewhere; perhaps around the house, across the lawn, over the concrete path, under the clothesline with flapping socks, past the dogs, and in to an environment of strange things the horse has not seen before. We are not only leading the horse but also giving it mental stimulation.

It has been demonstrated with experimental animals, and observed from babies kept in institutions (like hospitals), that lack of sensory stimulation impairs intelligence. Although no one has set up an experiment to show that horses in a mentally enriched environment have superior intelligence to those reared in a mentally deprived environment, this has been frequently shown with smaller animals.

> When the performance of jungle-born and laboratory-reared monkeys was compared on a variety of tasks requiring a wide range of cognitive abilities, the wild monkeys were superior in every test. Numerous studies

> are also cited where animals reared in an enriched or rich home environment were more successful problem solvers than those reared in impoverished environments or in laboratory cages. Rats reared in a free environment with 'playthings' were better problem solvers than rats reared in other conditions.[30]

We can infer from these studies that horses reared with other horses in a free and enriched environment (like a large paddock which offers variety and interest), if given the extra stimulation of owners who continually expand their mental horizons, will be more intelligent than a horse that never leaves its paddock or continually lives in a stable or yard.

7

THE IMPORTANCE OF HABIT

We shape our lives in many ways, through planned and unplanned actions: through choice and chance. The repetition of these actions, whether they are consciously intended or not, frequently becomes a habit.

A lot of our habits are created by biological needs, like eating and sleeping; or social needs like working and cleaning our teeth; or psychological needs like being with family and friends. So that a large part of every day is not determined by thought at all, it more or less just happens because of habit.

Horses are very much creatures of habit, too, but to an even greater degree; and like us, can form both good and bad habits. Good habits contribute to a horse's physical and psychological well-being; whereas bad habits frequently impair the horse's health or behaviour in some way.

Wild horses normally establish beneficial daily routines of regular eating, sleeping, and exercise which favour their digestion, health, and peace of mind. Bad habits in horses are usually caused by their association with people, and can form as a result of inadequate care and poor handling.

Additionally, training and riding a horse teaches it a whole range of new habits in relation to its work and us. In fact, training horses is all about habits: good training consists of teaching a horse a whole series of good habits; whereas a poor trainer teaches a horse some bad habits too.

For both us and the horse there are many advantages in forming habits. The habit of a daily routine gives a comfortable feeling, a feeling of emotional reassurance, of security. Habits provide the reassurance of familiarity, not just for the sequence of the day's events, but for all sorts of minor incidents that occur – like making a pot of tea; or for the horse, the way down the river bank so that it can drink the water. When we do things by habit we do not have to think about them, so there is no cause for anxiety. We avoid the stresses of decision and indecision. We are comfortable in ourselves.

Whatever we do with a horse from the beginning of its life will influence the creation of habits or forms of behaviour which it may well keep for the rest of its life. So our care and management of the young horse will affect not only how the horse relates to people, but whether the horse relates to its environment in a way that is constructive or destructive to the horse itself.

Every year when the mares come to stud, there are always a few who we initially think are quite sensible and intelligent but who then surprise us by behaving as if they are totally brainless!

It starts to rain, and it not only rains but it pours. In addition it is freezing cold, and the mares are not wearing rugs because they have foals at foot. The mare stands in the rain, cold and shivering, with no thought of going into the comfortable stable that is in her yard.

However, for the foal, providing that it is not extremely young, it is quite different! It has never been in the rain before and has not developed a habit of accepting the discomfort of being in the rain. Distressed by the cold it eventually leaves its mother's side and finds the warmth and comfort of the dry stable. Incredibly, it may not be until several hours later that mum follows her baby inside!

Probably these seemingly unintelligent mares were unable to find shelter in such weather when they were young, and now as older horses they put up with such conditions out of habit – a habit that is not conducive to the best health of the horse.

Horses learn new things easily when they are young; it is actually easier for them to learn new things than it is for older horses. There are two reasons for this. Firstly, a young horse may not have formed a habit of accepting things as they are and automatically always behaving in the same way. Secondly, because the horse is not locked into a certain form of behaviour by habit, it will have more flexibility of mind about doing new things and it will be more easily motivated to learn something different.

Every summer and autumn horses are plagued by bot-flies. Many older horses will just stand and try and drive the bot away by striking at it with their feet. Some will even pretend to ignore it. Not so with the foals. Although they will gallop around trying to get rid of the bot-fly, they seem to quickly discover that the bot will not follow them into the dense shade of a shelter shed or stable.

Foals who have learnt to evade bot-flies in such a way, will continue to do so as adult horses if they have access to shelter. Older horses who don't try and run away from bot-flies, usually have not had the use of shelter sheds when they were young, so have formed the habit of no longer attempting to evade these injurious insects.

As we have seen, the establishment of a habit can create a situation where a horse refuses to think – irrespective of how intelligent a horse may be, and even if solving the problem is in the horse's own interests. This became even more apparent to us when we tried to devise an intelligence test for horses.

We wanted to check the accuracy of an intelligence test for horses, so we tried it out on six horses of known intelligence: three stallions and three mares. All six horses were broken in, and we felt we knew how intelligent they were from their previous speed of learning new things. Additionally, the horses were usually fed their dinner of oats in a bucket placed inside a motor-car tire (so that they were less likely to spill it). Frequently when the horses had finished eating they would get the bucket out of the tire and search for any grain that might have spilled underneath.

So, to test their intelligence we decided to show each horse a plate of oats, and while it was still watching to place the food inside the ring of the tire with the *empty* feed bucket on top. We expected that the most intelligent horses would get the empty bucket off the top of the food in the shortest time.

The test was tried first on the horse who was regarded as having the lowest intelligence: a mare who lived around the family home. The test was carefully set up in front of her. She looked at it with considerable disbelief, picked up the bucket by its rim with her teeth, and tossed it aside: seven seconds! The test was hopelessly easy. The clever horses would do it in not time at all!

However, this proved not to be the case. The two other mares who lived in a paddock, took longer to solve the problem – one pawed the bucket out with her hoof, and the other removed it with her mouth. Of the stallions: one who spent the day out in a paddock, stuffed the bucket aside with his nose in the second fastest time; but the remaining two stallions, who lived in yards, completely failed the test – even when tested a second time. After a minute or two, they just walked away in disgust.

The test had obviously failed to give a true assessment of the intelligence of the horses. The two stallions who could not even do the test had previously shown themselves to be intelligent by their rapid ability to learn when they were broken in. The only reasonable conclusion appeared to be that because the two stallions lived in yards, and at that time were not being ridden, they consequently had a life that demanded virtually no decision making at all – their days were so dominated by habit that they had become completely unable to think.

Older horses get locked into habits. Thus we need to be especially careful what we do with young horses so that the habits they establish are in their interests and not to their detriment. We've considered the advantages of foals learning about shelter, some other habits of importance concern food.

Foals at a very early age start to copy their mothers and to nibble grass. Then, if the mares are given hay and grain the foals again copy their mothers and learn to eat the new food. So very early in a horse's life it establishes eating habits, and the horse may be very reluctant to change these habits when it is mature. So horses that are not fed grain when they are young, may not only grow less than their genetic potential, but may also suffer other disadvantages when they are older.

> Minyip was a wild mare who had been rescued from near starvation by a kind lady. Shortly after her rescue she had a foal, and her owner decided to put the mare back in foal again.
>
> However, it was a year of drought, and at the stud all the mares were given daily feeds of oats and hay to keep them in good condition; but Minyip, due to long habit, refused to eat anything but the poorest hay. Consequently, the mare and foal dropped rapidly in condition. It was only after a couple of weeks that Minyip deigned to eat alfalfa – which probably saved the lives of both horses. However, she never once attempted to nibble at her daily offering of oats in all the eight weeks she spent at the stud.

Horses and people who are stressed are extraordinarily resistant to changing their eating habits. Starving people have frequently refused to eat food that is foreign to them, and horses will behave in the same way.

There are other times, too, aside from being a brood mare, when a horse has extra nutritional needs so it is just as well if the horse has learnt to eat and enjoy lucerne and grain.

A sick horse will not be interested in trying a new good quality food while it is ill and when it may really need it. It may even totally refuse to eat unless it *knows a familiar food to be especially nice* – and poor quality hay can never be put in that category.

Additionally, a horse that enjoys eating a wider range of foodstuffs – alfalfa, oats, horse mixes, apples, carrots, and so on – provides us with a larger range of inducements to motivate it to do what we want as well as rewards for when it does do what we ask.

Habits become such an integral part of a horse that the breaking of a habit, or the disruption of a routine, can cause the horse considerable distress.

> It was the first day of the show season, but most of the horses did not understand. Much to their surprise, when it was still pitch dark they were all disturbed by lights being turned on, the slamming of car doors, and their owners rushing around and shouting to each other with the raised voices of excitement and hurry.
>
> So here was everyone, but where was breakfast? And immediately the horses began to demand their food.
>
> The horses did not get breakfast that morning: everyone was too busy. Neither had they been given extra hay the night before.
>
> That evening when the people returned from the show, they found that one of their mares was lying dead in the paddock. Her long and anxious wait for breakfast had caused her so much stress, that she had developed colic and died.

There are other aspects to the care of our horse that can cause the horse to create habits which are very destructive to itself. We have seen that habits provide a horse with comfort: they lull anxiety. For this reason, if we keep a horse in conditions where it is continually bored and suffers lack of mental stimulation, the resulting anxiety may cause the horse to develop some very bad habits indeed.

The idea of boredom is not very distressing to us because if we are bored we can usually do something about it, and so can a horse in the wild. However, for a horse shut in a small yard, or especially a stable, boredom is very distressing as there is little it can do to break the monotony, and it will become anxious.

How does a horse deal with anxiety? Movement. Movement helps dissipate the unpleasant feeling of anxiety, but the stabled horse has little opportunity for movement. Perhaps it will play with its food bucket or water bin, dig holes, kick the walls, and chew the woodwork. However, it is repetitive movement that has the most soothing effect. We are aware of this in other situations, and so commonly rock the cradles and prams of babies. So the horse may rapidly learn to weave, crib-bite, or wind-suck. These three vices are universally regarded as so detrimental to a horse, and so incurable, that if one is detected in a horse soon after it has been sold at a reputable horse auction, it is grounds for its sale to be cancelled.

There are many other bad and destructive habits that a bored and lonely horse may learn. A bored or lonely horse may become so neurotic, that it chases itself around in circles, and in extreme cases may even bite its own legs and savage its own sides until they are raw and bleeding.

> Superspeed was a highly credentialed Thoroughbred stallion imported into Australia to be a commercial sire. He had virtually lived his entire life in a stable as he was 'far too valuable to run the risk of being out in a yard!' Due to such severe deprivation of mental stimulation, he had to continually wear an iron mask to prevent him from tearing strips off his own sides with his teeth.
>
> However, such treatment does nothing to alleviate the causes of such a bad habit, and no doubt increases the horse's anxiety to even higher levels. Superspeed never managed to serve many mares. He became ill, and eventually died from 'a twisted bowel', which frequently is another way of saying that a horse died from psychological stress.

If a horse does have to live in a yard or stable, it must have exercise every day. It is also a good idea to give it some toys.

Toys amuse a horse and so help to lessen the chances that the horse will form bad habits which are destructive to itself or its surroundings. They even help the horse to be happier and more sensible.

What sort of toys are suitable for a horse? For a horse in a yard, hessian sacks, large balls, a soft football, a length of hose, and plastic buckets and plastic garbage bins and lids, can all provide entertainment. A toy should not have sharp edges or be small enough to be swallowed or jammed in the throat, neither should it break or tear into dangerous pieces. Lengths of rope should be avoided. Although horses love chewing rope, there is a high risk that it could be swallowed. Many horses also enjoy having an empty, plastic cold-drink container hung in their stable for them to play with and chew; but such containers deteriorate quickly and need to be continually replaced before they become dangerous and bits of them are swallowed.

As we have seen, horses can learn some things very quickly, and once learnt it becomes a habit so they don't have to reconsider the matter each time it arises. This is of great advantage to good horse trainers, but a real bane to poor ones. A good horse trainer teaches a horse good habits so that it does what he wants it to do automatically, without it learning any undesirable behaviour or bad habits in the process; but a poor trainer often finds that his horses learn something unwanted at the same time. A horse can learn desirable behaviour in one lesson, but it can just as easily learn a bad habit.

'Ernie' had been around horses all his life. He knew he was a good horseman – no one had dared to tell him otherwise!

Ernie had a handsome black mare for sale that he had bred and broken in himself. By the time the girl who had rung in response to his advertisement had arrived on the scene, the horse was already bridled and saddled.

The girl rode the horse and liked it. So she paid for it on the spot and took it home.

The next day she decided to saddle the horse for a ride, but as the girth was being tightened the horse pulled back in great fear, broke its halter rope, and threw itself over backwards sending the saddle crashing to the ground.

Ernie, who regarded himself as an expert with horses, had never at any time reassessed his skills. He had never considered that tightening the girth to the tightest hole the first time the saddle was put on the horse's back could hurt and frighten the horse and make it 'girth shy' forever.

Ernie never would admit he had made a mistake with the horse.

'It was cheap at $600!' he growled.

Bad habits in horses are frequently created by people causing the horse anxiety. The horse that develops stable vices suffers the anxiety of enforced boredom: the riding horse's anxieties are usually due to the fear of pain caused by hurtful equipment, faulty training, or poor riding.

If the bad habit is to be cured its cause must be removed first of all. The stimulus (or pain) which causes the anxiety response (or bad habit) must be eliminated. So, if the horse rears or puts its tongue over the bit, the chances are that it has been hurt in the mouth by a rider with bad hands. This bad habit is not likely to be cured until the horse is ridden by someone with good hands who does not hurt the horse.

However, it is rarely that simple. Once the horse has been hurt, especially if the horse has been hurt more than once, the horse forms the bad habit in response to its *fear of pain*, and removing the pain does not remove the fear of pain. So everytime a bit is put in the horse's mouth it can trigger the fear of being hurt. Or if the horse has been jabbed in the mouth when it is being mounted, it goes on expecting pain in the mouth whenever it is mounted. Consequently it continues to put its tongue over the bit or to rear.

When a bad habit is well established anxiety alone may act as the stimulus. If the horse is taken to a show, or event, or some other unfamiliar place, its apprehension automatically increases. Then, when it is ridden in the showring, or it sees something possibly threatening, its anxiety peaks – it promptly stands on its hind legs or pulls its tongue back over the bit. So not only the pain has to be removed to cure the habit; but also the fear of pain, and anxiety as well.

Occasionally a horse starts some form of undesirable behaviour, such as putting its tongue over the bit, due to anxiety alone, and without it having been hurt; but we still have to cure the anxiety to prevent the unwanted behaviour developing into a habit.

Huckleberry Finn was a bay Thoroughbred gelding who was only four years old. He had already been to quite a number of shows where he competed in halter classes; but this was the first occasion where he was ridden in a saddle class.

His young rider, 'Wendy', saddled him up, and started to trot him around in the practice ring with a number of other horses. But what was that? Huckleberry's tongue was protruding out of the corner of his mouth and flapping in the breeze! His rider dismounted to check, and unbelievably it was true; although he had never before put his tongue over the bit.

So the bit was taken out of his mouth and put back in the proper place, and Wendy continued to calmly trot him around with the other horses; and Huckleberry kept putting his tongue over the bit again, and again, and again.

However, by the time Huckleberry's class was called some thirty minutes later, he had dissipated a lot of his anxiety through movement and was no longer putting his tongue over the bit. So he managed to compete with success.

The reduction of the horse's anxiety through movement and calm handling, not only solved the bit problem for that day but also prevented the horse from establishing an undesirable form of behaviour to present on other occasions when it felt anxious.

When we are handling a horse, especially a young one, we need to be careful that we don't do anything with it that could become a bad habit. Even doing something only once can be enough to train the horse to behave in a way we would rather it didn't!

If the horse suddenly starts bucking when we ride it, and we jump off and swat it with a cane; the horse will remember, but it may remember the wrong thing. So later when we want to dismount the horse won't let us. It will refuse to stand still because the last time we got off it was punished!

As we have just seen, bad habits can be dramatically reinforced with pain: one painful occurrence can be sufficient to make a permanent bad habit in a horse. So a horse that is roughly bridled may become 'head shy' and always throw its head when someone tries to put a bit in its mouth; or a horse that is galled by the saddle when it is initially broken in may always have a 'cold back' and buck; and a horse that has its girths thoughtlessly tightened immediately to the top hole may become 'girth shy'.

The best way to avoid bad habits is to anticipate the possibility of their occurrence and to be careful how we handle and train horses.

Horses are individuals and cannot all be trained in the same way. A trainer may frequently have to change a preconceived way of educating a horse to avoid some problem or bad habit that he or she 'senses' will arise.

'Habibi' was a pretty and correct Arabian mare, so her owner decided that she would be the showpony of her dreams; but she forgot about Habibi's temperament. Habibi was an impatient horse and was always in a hurry to do everything before she was even asked.

Conventional schooling in preparation for the show ring proved to be impossible. From the first time she was asked to canter a figure-of-eight she knew that one *always* cantered a figure-of-eight; and so when she was asked to trot one instead, she became increasingly anxious, excited, irrational, and disobedient. Her desire and anxiety to anticipate her rider's every request made her impossible to school in the restricted space of the dressage arena.

However, when she was schooled surreptitiously, without her realising it, by riding her in huge paddocks and along country roads; and asking her to change legs, diagonals, and paces in unfamiliar places, her anxiety was kept dormant. She eventually became quite well educated, without forming any bad habits – in spite of herself!

Although many bad habits are formed in horses due to anxiety, occasionally bad habits develop in horses where they receive some tangible reward for their actions, like avoiding work or stealing food.

Halima was an Arabian mare. She and her companion lived in a paddock of only a few acres and so required a daily feed of grain and hay. During the summer when there was not even a blade of green grass in the paddock, her feed of oats and other goodies became inordinately important to her, to the extent that one day when her dinner had not arrived at the usual time she began to paw at the fence in anxiety.

Unsurprisingly, she became caught in the wires, but her owner had seen what had happened, and immediately raced to the rescue. Fortunately Halima had enough sense not to panic, and just stood still until the offending wire was cut and she was released. However, she still had not been fed and so she started to paw at the fence again. Her owner rushed to bring her a bucket of oats before she should become entangled in the fence once again.

From that occasion Halima learnt that the fastest way to get a bucket of oats was to stand in the fence, and not even feeding excessive amounts of hay or removing the bottom two wires from the fence had the slightest effect in breaking this bad habit. Instead, a now very fat Halima would be found at all times of day, demanding oats, by standing deep in the fence with wires right up to her armpits!

The wires of the fence were eventually replaced with mesh, and Halima having tried once, and finding that her leg did not go through, ceased to paw at the fence for oats.

Some bad habits that horses acquire may be learnt 'passively': they are caused by faulty training or poor riding, and no one may be aware of them until the horse changes hands or gets a new rider. Such bad habits include the horse refusing to stand still while someone is trying to mount it, or the horse cantering on only one lead. Nevertheless, if at a later date someone should wish to cure the horse of such a bad habit they will find it difficult to do so.

Curing or modifying habits in a horse can be very hard. One of the problems with habits is that they become so ingrained, so much part of the horse, that to try and stop the habit may make the horse extremely anxious and resistant.

Worse, many bad habits can be especially difficult to cure because they are likely to have been created by anxiety in the first place, and trying to stop the habit increases the horse's anxiety. Anyone who has tried to alter their own habits, like going on a diet or giving up smoking, will realise the degree of ill-ease and anxiety it causes. So trying to break the habit actually increases the compulsion to smoke or to eat too much!

So what can we do about bad habits in horses? We can remove the cause of the habit, reduce the horse's anxiety, and try and establish other patterns of behaviour.

Honey was sweet and gentle from the day she was born, so it was rather a surprise when she came home from the horse breaker with a completely changed personality. When her owner tried to get on, she crossed her jaws, and flung herself up on to her hind legs, wild-eyed and distraught; and no amount of reassurance, leaving the reins completely slack, or having another person hold her made any difference.

Her owner felt she had neither the skill nor the courage to ride her. So instead, a confident horseperson was engaged to do battle with Honey, but after riding her for two weeks Honey's behaviour was worse.

It became obvious that pushy-aggression had to be replaced by calm, reassurance, and bribery. So Honey's owner decided to get a helper to hold a bucket of oats and alfalfa chaff for Honey to eat while she herself mounted her, and this was done in such a relaxed and calm fashion that Honey also remained calm and went on eating.

After several days of this treatment, Honey became less anxious and forgot her bad habits of rearing and crossing her jaws; and she eventually became quite a pleasant horse to ride.

Frequently a horse that habitually rears when it is mounted is also likely to rear every time it feels anxious, such as when it is passed by a truck on the road or it sees a monster; but it is especially likely to rear when it is asked to stand still.

Play For Keeps was an ex-racehorse, who always stood on her hind legs every time her rider asked her to halt.

So for several weeks she was never asked to stand still with a rider on her back. If she was out with other riders on the road, and they stopped to alter stirrups or to open gates, she was walked up and down the road until the others were ready.

Gradually it became possible to stop her for a few seconds, and then to ask her to start walking again before her anxiety rose and she reared.

As time passed she could be halted for longer and longer intervals, and eventually she forgot her rearing habit altogether.

Bad habits in horses are often triggered by association with something else or by expectation. A horse that has been continually galloped by one owner, is not going to change its expectations of being ridden just because it has been bought by someone who wants to travel at a more sedate speed! The new owner may find to their dismay, that they not only have a horse who is a perpetual puller, but one who also refuses to learn to travel more slowly.

The 'cure' to all pullers, we are frequently told, is to let the horse gallop, and when it is tired to push it on and on and on! 'And never again will it pull!'

Hazar was an Arabian stallion, and an incessant puller. So he was a worthwhile subject for the 'cure'.

He wanted to gallop! Good! So he and his rider galloped up a long hill and then down a longer hill and then up another hill and so on without a break for eight exhausting miles, and the more his rider puffed and gasped for breath, the more he enjoyed himself and the faster he went!

The next day, instead of being calm and gentle to ride, he was frightfully excited and pulling much harder than ever before. Galloping the previous day had reinforced the expectation of doing it again.

It took many days of calm slow work to reduce his expectation of galloping and consequently reduce his degree of pulling. Pulling was associated with expectation of speed: if his expectation of speed was reduced, so was the pulling.

Irrespective of whether a horse's bad habit is associated with anxiety or expectation, it is often best dealt with by avoiding the situation in which it appears; until the horse's anxiety or expectation is reduced, and a new habit of desirable behaviour has begun to form.

Some horses buck or rear, and may do so for any of a large number of reasons. They include poor handling and breaking in, anxiety or excitement, resentment of a particular form of work or a rider who bumps up and down on the horse's back, or, of course, the horse may just simply prefer not to be ridden! If the horse is not provoked into bucking or rearing, it is likely to give up such a habit if the rider remains calm and doesn't fall off. However, many horses that buck seem to pick their victims; they may always be well-behaved with a competent rider and only buck when their rider has less ability.

So sometimes a horse may only have a bad habit in relation to a certain rider, and in that case it will be the rider who will need the extra training.

At a top English riding academy all the pupils, many of whom were experienced and proficient riders, rode the academy's schooled horses.

One day a huge prancing, stomping, snorting horse, with the strength and energy of a steam train, was brough to the academy for schooling. Only one rider, a slightly built girl called 'Evelyn', was considered to be sufficiently capable to ride this powerful and frightening horse, which she did to the admiration and applause of everyone watching.

Next day, in her usual riding class, Evelyn was given one of the beginners' ponies to ride; not because she had become 'big-headed' over night, but because her instructor had spotted one weakness in her riding. He knew that this particular pony would test that weakness and so would help Evelyn to learn to correct her problem.

So everyone was terribly surprised, except for the instructor, when Evelyn's pony shot out of the ring at an extended trot and succeeded in taking her all the way back to the stables!

Thus to a large extent a horse is what it is through the formation of many habits. As we have so much control in forming a horse's habits it is up to us to teach it good ones; and not through our own lack of thought or knowledge, or want of kindness and sensitivity, impair the horse; or even worse, teach it such bad habits that its life will be a misery to itself or others.

8

INSTINCT AND MOTIVATION

Most of the time horses are fairly obliging creatures, so we tend to take it for granted that they should do what we ask of them. However, every now and then we try to do something with a horse who says, 'I won't!', and it is then we begin to wonder why horses do anything for us at all!

The real difficulty in training horses to do what we want, is that we are trying to teach them things that are in conflict with their own instincts.

A horse's natural instincts are not very useful to us, unlike those of a dog. Guard dogs follow their natural instinct to bark at strangers; cattle and sheep dogs use their instinct to chase game; retrievers naturally help those who like to shoot; and most pet dogs share with us their desire to be companionable.

However, for a horse to be of value it has to be trained, unless it is to be used for breeding purposes alone. Untrained it has no use.

The horse has to learn to accept the leadership of another species: us. It must accept commands from people, rather than follow its own instinct or that of another horse. It has to learn to accept being tethered, when every instinct tells it to fight for freedom. It has to learn to accept equipment and a rider on its back, when instinct tells it that it could be a predatory tiger. It is not naturally calm and sensible; the slightest alarm or hint of danger, the softest rustle or unexpected movement, triggers fright and flight.

So it is necessary to change or modify some of the horse's natural instincts by what is usually described as 'breaking it in!' However, the 'breaking in' often leaves a lot to be desired.

> Every year on the 'P-Q-Ranch', the cowboys would round up the mustangs in the hills and herd them into a corral, and the best of the two-year-olds were chosen to break in as stock horses. (The hooves on older horses had usually deteriorated beyond repair.) The horses were immobilised with ropes; saddled and bridled; then mounted and released. Then away they would go, bucking in terror and anger until exhausted. When the horse stopped bucking it was regarded as 'broken in'.
>
> It did not seem to be a very satisfactory process: every year they repeated the same method, and they never produced any horses that they considered worthwhile.

There are now growing numbers of people who realise that there are better ways to break in horses, and that it is quite unnecessary and even undesirable to enter into combat or competition with the horse.

How then are we to teach a horse to do what we want it to do? The answer is to motivate the horse into doing what we ask through positive rewards.

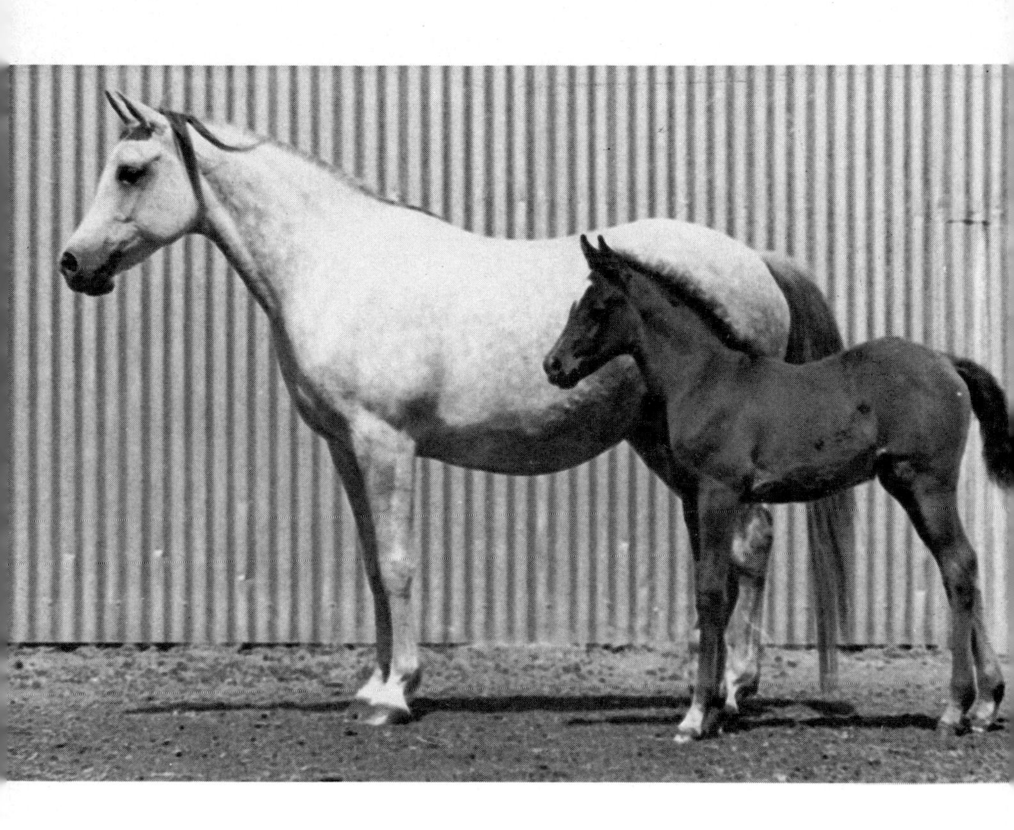

21 The foal copies its mother, and so in this case is not learning the habit of running away from people. (Chapter 7)

22 Horses that live in yards benefit from being able to play with 'toys'. Plastic garbage bins are a favourite toy. (Chapter 7)

23 Greed can be a powerful force in motivating a horse to do what we want. This colt who had never been in a horse float before was happy to walk straight in for a reward of food. (Chapter 8)

24 Horses often like as companions those of the same colour. This black pony and black draught horse have become special friends, despite the disparity of their breeds. (Chapter 9)

25 The chestnut mare who has put her ears back and pulled up her nostrils is telling the white stallion quite clearly that she has no interest in him. (Chapter 9)

26 Foals should be caressed and held in our arms right from the very beginning of their lives. (Chapter 10)

27 Well-handled foals are more likely to be sociable and friendly than their neglected counterparts. (Chapter 12)

28, **29**, **30** and **31** Taming the older foal. (Chapter 10)

28 The handler makes herself as small and unthreatening as possible, and lets the foal approach her. Gradually the foal comes to like being gently scratched on the chest.

29 The foal likes being scratched, and accepts the handler slowly standing upright.

30 The top of the wither is often an itchy spot, and the foal learns to accept the handler standing in other positions.

31 The foal accepts its first real discipline of being held.

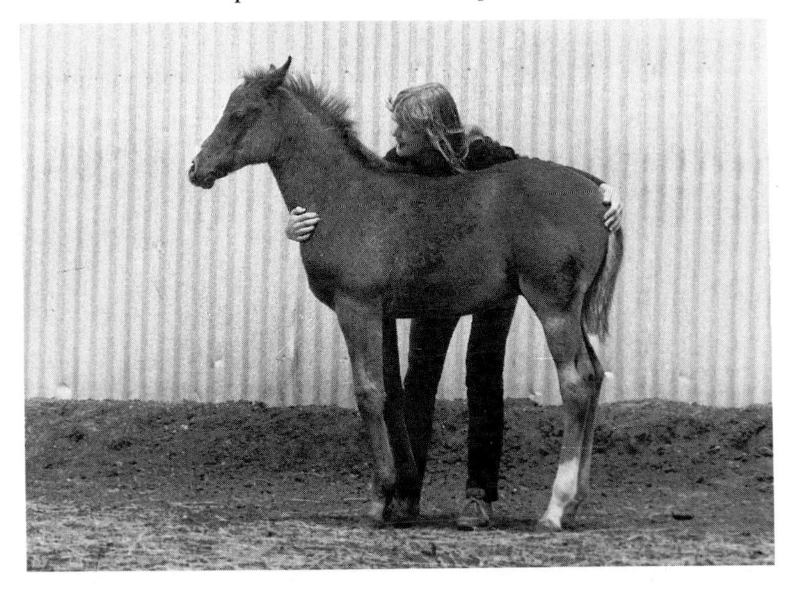

32 This old stallion, with heart trouble, still needs regular exercise to keep him happy and to avoid colic. (Chapter 11)

33 A showhorse should have an attractive head. (Chapter 12)

34 The best showhorses display a look of quality. (Chapter 12)

35 Horses need the inclination to do something to do it well. This unbroken Arabian colt shows a willingness to jump. (Chapter 12)

36 No inclination to jump! This Arabian filly wouldn't even step across the log for a bucket of food! (Chapter 12)

37 *Rahalima* – dream horse.

38 *Rahalima* and the author.

'Cathy' worked at one of the better riding schools. 'Worked' was not really the right word as she suffered from ill-health, and any physical job required a lot of effort; but she liked the horses and spent a lot of time talking to them, and scratching and stroking them. As the horses always seemed to be quieter and more sensible when she was around, the owner of the riding school was happy for her to be there.

One day the owner was agitated because an unexpectedly large number of students had arrived, and on seeing Cathy nearby, he suddenly decided that she could bring up an extra horse from the paddock and also saddle and bridle it.

Cathy went and caught the horse and brought it up to the stables and began to groom it. As it was rather fidgety, which made it difficult for her, she gave it some alfalfa hay so that it would be content and stand still. So she groomed the horse, and saddled the horse, very slowly and carefully as she had only really watched other people do it before. Tentatively she did up the girths only one hole at the time, and kept running her fingers underneath them to make sure that she had not pinched any skin or caught any hair.

She was not very sure about putting the bridle on, but the horse had its mouth so full of food that it did not really seem to notice the bit go in, and although it ducked its head a little when she tried to pull its ears under the top of the bridle, it did not really mind when she tried threading them through with their tips going first; and the whole time she was talking quietly to the horse, and stroking the horse, and the horse was munching away.

Some time later the owner suddenly remembered Cathy. He found her leading a small child around on the horse's back. Not very surprising really, except that the horse had not been broken in – Cathy had the wrong horse! 'You stupid twit!' he said good-humouredly to her later; but she had proved that she was not stupid at all!

Cathy had very successfully motivated the horse into doing what she wanted, without having an argument with the horse in any way.

The intelligent trainer modifies a horse's 'un-useful' instincts with positive rewards (those that give the horse pleasure), instead of trying to change the horse's instincts with force.

Horses, like people, can be motivated to do things for us in a number of different ways, and the best way to motivate them is through their instinctive needs.

Horses need food. However, most horses will eat more food than physically necessary for them if they are given the opportunity to do so, because as we all know eating is a pleasure.

This desire for excess food we may as well call greed. The greediness of horses differs from individual to individual, so that some will really only eat a maintenance ration whilst others would eat enough to sink a ship if we gave them the chance. So greed can be a powerful force in motivating many horses to do what we want if we reward them with food.

Mahbub was a purebred Arabian mare who had never left the property where she was born. When she was three years old she was broken in. Although she accepted her training and new way of life with complete decorum and never a hint of resistance, it was quite a different story when she was taken out on the road for the first time and asked to walk over a wooden bridge. 'No', she said. 'It is too dangerous to walk on wooden boards. It is impossible!' And she planted her four feet firmly in the middle of the road and refused to budge. Although most horses will follow a companion over these little country bridges, she could not be induced to even follow her best friend, and neither did a good swat with a cane on her rear-end improve the situation! All pleadings and cajolings, stroking and reassurance, fell on deaf ears. The bridge could not be crossed.

The next day the same ride was repeated; but this time Mahbub's rider carried reinforcement in the form of a small bag of Mahbub's favourite food. When Mahbub was offered the food in return for putting her feet on the bridge, the bridge rapidly became less frightening and drew in its horns and fangs and Mahbub crossed over. Mahbub was rewarded with more food, and again the next few times she crossed (to reinforce the establishment of a good habit). When she realised that she had managed to achieve the seemingly impossible without being hurt; her confidence, pride, and self-esteem dramatically increased, so much so, that she became keen to be the lead horse over any and every wooden bridge!

Horses can be motivated by their own pride and self-respect. Many horses learn to enjoy the pride of achievement providing they are introduced to the activity without being hurt. Many competition horses, like jumpers and racehorses, enjoy their success.

Other horses can take pride in more abstract achievements. A stock horse may enjoy his masterly control of cattle; a milkman's horse may enjoy his seeming independence negotiating city streets alone while his driver takes milk into each house; and a good child's pony will take pride in looking after its young rider. However, it is all a matter of temperament as well as how the task is presented to the horse: some horses get a great sense of achievement in dumping their riders on the ground instead.

Horses can also be motivated by their need for companions. The need for companions is a very strong instinct in horses, and is what we should expect in herd animals. The herd provides many necessities for a horse's well-being: companionship, affection, a sense of belonging, and security. So it is not surprising that a horse's need to be with a special companion or with other horses is very intense, and most solitary horses will try and join up with others if given the chance.

Right from the earliest days of training a horse, we use its need for a companion to motivate it to do what we want.

We teach the foal to lead by having someone walk its mother ahead of it. We encourage foals to accept weaning by giving them companion foals to help make easier their loss. We train a horse to do something new by having a companion horse for it to follow. We educate a horse to accept the worries of the road by having an experienced companion horse (preferably a friend who is higher in the pecking order of the herd) for the novice to tail or have at its side to help shield it from the traffic.

The presence and reassurance of the companion horse helps the novice horse to form good habits and to do the right thing naturally. However, more than this, the experienced companion horse can not only help a novice horse to accept new things without fear or fuss, but can also help it to enjoy them. If we are taking a horse over low jumps for the first time, or even just over poles on the ground, and the trained horse is jumping them ahead, our novice is likely to follow its example and, providing that it is not hurt, enjoy itself too. Thus the enjoyment of jumping becomes the reward, and the horse being motivated to jump will not be dependent upon a companion.

Less obviously, our praise can motivate the horse. A

horse's instinctive needs for companionship and affection are normally satisfied by other horses; but when we handle and train a horse it will also turn to us for satisfaction of these needs. The horse will learn to need approval, affection, and caresses from us. So it may perform well to try to please us, providing we praise and pet it and tell it how clever it is in return. (Everyone knows that it is not much fun working for someone who does not appreciate our efforts!)

The horse's need for acceptance and belonging makes it want to be part of the herd, and its personality will determine its position in the pecking order of the herd. Horses transfer their concept of hierarchy to people. So when we handle a horse, if it respects us, and feels that we are superior in the pecking order, it may accept our authority when we ask it to do something.

Such respect is an important part of our relationship with a horse. If the horse learns to respect us, and to trust and have confidence in us, it will learn to accept reassurance from *us*. It will not be totally dependent on other horses to feel secure. It will accept us as 'herd leader' and its instinct to shy or bolt will be reduced if we ourselves remain calm. It is then that we can ride the novice horse out on the road by itself. Its instincts have been modified to accept some of its emotional needs – security, companionship, and affection – from a person instead of a horse.

Horses can also be motivated by their need for sensory stimulation. Many have a low tolerance for boredom and for repetitive work, and often deliberately seek excitement. So sometimes a horse can be motivated to do one thing it does not like if it learns that the activity will be followed by something it does like. The horse may not like being schooled, but it may do its best if it knows it will have an enjoyable cross-country ride afterwards.

However, boredom is not always a bad thing: it can be a useful pacifier for 'highly strung' horses. Some horses repond to everything that is strange with rapidly increasing tension and emotion. The unusual becomes exciting, and the exciting rapidly becomes frightening! Such nervous horses when out on the road see all sorts of things which incite this escalating emotion. If the rider can impart a feeling of complete boredom or intense calm to the horse, its emotions may subside.

'Mark' was a self-made man. The many rolls of fat that collared his neck, and his huge 'executive' size suit that covered his corpulent body proclaimed the fact; but what was worse, he also had an over-inflated self-esteem to match!

Mark had a girlfriend, Sally, who loved riding. However, Mark did not like Sally to enjoy herself without him, so one day he decided to accompany her on a ride – although he had never ridden before.

When they arrived at the country property for the ride, and the stable-man saw Mark's arrogant over-confidence he decided that here was a man for whom life had been too easy and something needed to be done about it!

Instead of bringing out the quiet cob which had already been prepared for Mark to ride, he brought out a very handsome chestnut Thoroughbred mare who was of a nervous and highly-strung nature. The horse's nostrils were already flared, and the veins stood out clearly in her smooth and satiny skin.

When Sally saw the beautiful horse she was filled with dismay. She knew that she would be unable to deter Mark from riding it: it was all too obviously the most glamourous horse in the establishment!

Mark was hoisted on to the horse, where he sat, bored and passive, completely unperturbed, with the reins dangling slackly from one hand.

Unfortunately this story does not have the expected ending. Mark did not fall off! His boredom, quiet confidence and easy calm influenced the horse to such an extent, that although Mark knew nothing about riding, the horse just went quietly along with the others as if it had never shied or spooked at anything in all its life!

Although calmness from an unthinking rider may help the horse, unkindness certainly will not.

As we have said earlier, the horse that is trained with painful stimuli, particularly in the absence of positive rewards, will become anxious and beset by problems.

This does not mean that we never punish a horse, because we must if it tries to kick our head in or chomp our flesh with its teeth; especially as nasty horses can become dangerous horses. However, neither should we punish a horse if we are stupid enough to feed it our hand or walk up behind it and let it mistake us for another horse!

There are many ways to motivate a horse to do what we want, and usually we use several ways together. Horses, like people, have to be in the right mood to learn. They have many emotions and some of them are just not conducive to learning anything at all. A horse needs some degree of mental stimulation to learn. If the horse is half asleep, or bored, it is not going to learn very much or even take much notice of its trainer. Too much emotion can also make an impossible situation for learning.

Whatever motivation we use, it is important not to make the horse upset, anxious, frightened, or angry; because next time we try and do whatever it is, the horse will remember and say to itself, 'This makes me frightened!', and will promptly become anxious and difficult again. *Horses remember the emotion associated with something*. So if a terrifying tree stump at the side of the road makes the horse shy, and the rider decides to motivate the horse to pass it by being calm, reassuring, and even bored, the horse is likely to only look at the offending stump the next day. If, on the other hand, the rider decides to motivate the horse to pass the stump with a sharp cut of the cane, the chances are that in the future the horse will associate the tree stump with pain and fright and will promptly shy again.

Another factor in motivating horses is the temperament or personality of the horse. It is a mistake to expect all horses to react in the same way to a given situation, or even to expect all horses of the same breed to have the same temperament.

Darky and Tommy were two Shetland ponies of unrelated breeding. They were both small, black, affectionate, intelligent, and three years old; but there their similarity ended, because they both used their intelligence to gain different ends and were motivated by quite different forces.

Darky was perfectly sweet to handle, and to saddle and to mount; and even to ride for the first ten minutes or so, but after that he decided, 'enough is enough'. So he sat down! His rider would then realise that perhaps it was a better idea to keep him moving rather than standing around chatting to Mum. Goody! Action! He would head straight for the nearest and prickliest hawthorn hedge and attempt to scrape his rider from his back. His rider then learnt to keep him out in open spaces and also away from trees with low hanging branches!

Problem solved? Pony and rider would canter serenely up the hill in the open paddock, but instead of stopping at the top, Darky would gallop madly down the other side, buck at the bottom, and if his passenger was still aboard he would collapse in a heap and roll; which made it rather impossible for a rider, terrified or not, to remain on his back a moment longer! Darky used his considerable intelligence to outwit his young riders and to avoid working. His temperament was too unwilling for a child to be able to motivate him.

Tommy was perfectly sweet and easy to handle and saddle too, but unlike Darky, he was perfect to ride all the time. He used his considerable intelligence to steal food (despite being rather fat already). If he was brought in from the paddock and left to graze on the succulent front lawn, it was always a surprise to find how quickly he disappeared. He had gone to search for tastier treats he believed to be hidden in the rubbish bins that were behind the back door. If he was not there, disaster had struck!

Tommy had let himself inside the house (the front door had a lever handle), and there Tommy would be in the dining room munching away at a vase of flowers or a bowl of fruit. On other occasions (it was hard to remember to keep the front door always locked with a key), Tommy would be found in the kitchen trying out different varieties of cheese, which he declared were all delicious, except for the Danish Blue!

Needless to say, Tommy had a personality that meant he could be motivated to do just about anything for food.

There are many things that we do with horses which cannot be much fun for them. However, we can teach them to accept the more tiresome aspects of their lives with positive rewards like food, so that good habits are established and the horse then does the right thing automatically.

Additionally, although we may have to motivate the

horse to enjoy being ridden, which requires a certain amount of commonsense and consideration on our part, the horse that enjoys its work will in turn reward us by being a greater pleasure to handle and ride.

9

SUCCESSFUL BREEDING

If we have some understanding of horses; of their needs, temperament, and emotions; it is not only easier for us to care for them and to work them satisfactorily, but also to be more successful breeding them.

Thousands of stallions of many different breeds stand at public stud. Although many of these stud farms are managed very well, there are many that are not – which accounts for the low national percentage of mares that are successfully put in foal each year. Only about fifty per cent of mares sent to stud are returned in foal – a very low figure when compared to the ninety per cent rate estimated for herds of wild horses.

All too often people regard breeding horses as a purely mechanical business or mathematical process: put two horses together and you get a third! This consideration of only the anatomy and physiology of horses results in a lot of needlessly barren mares and disappointed mare owners each year.

Mona was said to be a non-breeder, although she had produced a number of foals on the stud farm where she was born, before being sold for a very high price.

However, at her new home she failed to get into foal, even after several years. With the result that the stud manager lost his job, her owner lost a lot of money, and Mona, now a scarecrow of her former self, nearly lost her life through neglect and starvation.

Once again she was sold, but this time at public auction and for a fraction of her former price. Her new owners, not unnaturally, thought that if they fattened her up she would return to normal fertility. This they did, but Mona continued to refuse the advances of the stallion. The vet was called in, but his advice and injections had no effect. In spite of being teased every evening when her owners came home from work, she continued to find the stallion insufferable!

The stallion was a well-mannered horse, and used to both hand and paddock serving, so he and Mona were turned out in the paddock together; but each horse pretended that the other was invisible. They grazed as far away from each other as possible. After all, he knew when he wasn't wanted! Why should he risk being kicked to pieces?

One warm sunny day, when the sun was warm on everyone's backs, and the lush green grass was studded with yellow and pink spring flowers, it was decided to bring Mona and the stallion into the yards and to tease them properly there. When the human introduction service reacquainted them, both horses rather surprisingly said, 'Yes please!' And Mona subsequently had the first foal she had had for many years. Thereafter it was realised that she had to be hand teased and at no other time than at midday and with the sun on her back!

Although we would not expect wild horses to have as many psychological problems as domestic horses, it would seem reasonable to expect stud farms to achieve a higher success rate than Mother Nature does in the wild. In a well run stud the horses should be better fed and healthier. Genuine breeding problems can often be remedied by a good horse veterinarian. And the stallion can even be given physical assistance. If the mare is nearly as tall as the stallion, or even taller, she can be held still and positioned on a suitably sloping piece of land to make it easier for him. The usual practice of bandaging the mare's tail also makes it easier for the stallion and protects him from injury.

Additionally, on a stud farm all mares that come into season can be served. In the wild some mares may miss out, due to the bossiness of other mares higher in the pecking order being possessive of either the stallion or the mare. In the rare case where a mare that is genuinely in season refuses at all times to accept the stallion's advances, she can be hobbled and served.

The difficulty of domestic horses having considerably more psychological problems in relation to breeding than wild horses, is annulled by the perceptive stud manager finding a way around the difficulty.

Federico Tesio has often been described as the greatest racehorse breeder of this century. From a relatively small stud and limited financial resources he produced some of the greatest racehorses, sires, and broodmares of all time, including such horses as Nearco and Ribot. He was regarded as a genius and as having a 'sixth sense' in relation to horses.

At one time Tesio had a successful racing stallion called Brunelleschi, which he sold to the Department of Agriculture as a sire. The Department booked in forty-five mares to be served by the stallion, but when the first glossy maiden mare was brought to him, he only showed a flicker of interest before he turned his back on her. The studmaster was somewhat surprised, but realising that the stallion had never served a mare before, brought him 'a voluptuous matron, rich in worldly experience',[31] but to no avail. And so it continued; not one of the forty-five glamourous mares could tempt him.

A veterinary surgeon was called to administer stimulants and aphrodisiascs to the stallion, but he remained indifferent to the mares.

Eventually the stud master decided that as the stallion had proved useless they had no other option than to geld the horse and send him to a cavalry regiment as a common troop horse.

However, before this fate befell Brunelleschi, Tesio arrived on the scene. 'Go and fetch the ugliest, dirtiest, most disreputable-looking mare you can lay your hands on', he ordered. 'If necessary plaster her with mud yourselves, but make sure she is good and dirty. Then go away and leave her alone with Brunelleschi.'

Then Brunelleschi, seeing that this dirty mare was quite different from all the beautiful ladies he had been made to ignore during his years as a racehorse, wondered whether he might, after all . . . He curled up his nose, tasting her delicious smell in the air, took a furtive check behind him just to make sure that no one was watching, and served her! This new experience for him was such a success, that when offered a second mare some hours later, she was taken with equal delight.

Brunelleschi eventually served all the mares and Tesio himself was pronounced to be 'The Wizard of Dormello'.

Many studs fail to get as high a percentage as possible of mares in foal due to a number of causes: psychological problems with mares and stallions; the stud manager's lack of basic physiological and behavioural knowledge of mares and stallions; inadequate or incompetent teasing of the mares; and failure to use the services of a veterinarian to correct genuine breeding problems.

Psychological problems of the mare

Stress

Horses that are stressed are less likely to get into foal. The stress can range from overwork in a racehorse to underfeeding a brood mare; from loss of a special companion horse to separation from a trusted owner. Whatever the cause may be, the stress is doubled if the horse has had a background of deprivation. So the mares that are most likely to be difficult to get into foal, are wild horses and riding school horses which have been rescued from near starvation.

Culture shock

When a mare is sent to stud it may at first be a very stressful experience for her, not necessarily in physical terms but mainly in psychological ways. She will have lost the security of all with which she is familiar: her companion horses, her normal environment, known people, and her usual food. The chances are that even the water and the grasses in the pasture may be different from what she is used to. Although for some horses the stress may be fairly minimal, as exhibited by the 'professional' brood mares who accept going to a different stud each year without too much anxiety, for many other mares the stress may be considerable. These mares may reveal their anxiety by eating poorly, by listlessness and depression, or by 'stewing' around and running up and down the fence.

However, frequently the mare's stress is not so obvious, and we may only become aware of it when a horse whose reproductive system has been cycling normally suddenly becomes disrupted. 'She came into season this morning!' a mare owner may say on delivering a mare to a stud a few hours later. But when the mare is teased thoroughly that evening and the following day she may make it quite clear that she is no longer in oestrus. Or, as is fairly common, mares that go to stud may fail to conceive the first time they come into season and are served, but get into foal the next time they are served three weeks later without any veterinary intervention.

Most mares settle in within a few weeks and their reproductive systems return to normal.

So when a mare comes to stud, because it is desirable to get her into foal as soon as possible, it is necessary to get her to accept her new environment as fast as possible and with minimal anxiety.

The first step is to feed her something she will enjoy eating. We like to give a visiting mare some good quality hay including some alfalfa and a dinner of oats providing she is not too fat. To be offered food in any home or in any language is reassuring. The horse feels it too. And eating is not only pleasant, but it also has a comforting tranquillising effect! The horse will be reassured.

The second step is to choose a suitable companion or companions for the mare. If she is isolated on her own she may be too stressed to cycle normally; and if her companions are not chosen with care, she may be stressed or physically injured. So we match horses for temperament and avoid putting gentle horses with overtly quarrelsome ones. Additionally, we like to put together mares of the same breed or colour, as horses frequently choose companions that look like themselves or their dams.

Mares with foals are given a separate paddock. Mares without foals, companion mares or brood mares that have not yet foaled, may share the same paddock only if they are lower in the pecking order to the mares with foals. Occasionally, a mare who has not got a foal may attack a foal that belongs to a mare lower in the social heirarchy; and some mares get so excited at the sight of another mare's foal that they will try to take possession of it.

The mare is never put straight out into the paddock. She is wormed, and put in a yard adjoining the paddock which is fenced in mesh (so a horse can't kick through) and has a rail top. Here she can then meet her future companions in safety. When the horses show some degree of acceptance of each other, usually only a day or two later, they are then put together.

Even if the visiting mares are to be kept in yards with shelters or stables (possibly for greater safety and easier handling of the foal), it is necessary to have a suitable companion in the adjoining yard.

Anxiety due to lack of feed

The mares need to be well fed. Good quality feed will play a large part in helping a mare to settle in, and will give her a feeling of psychological wellbeing, which will be reflected in her general health. Vets agree that mares at stud that are maintained on 'a rising plane of nutrition' are likely to respond with increased fertility and likelihood of the mare getting into foal.

The opposite situation is also true. If a horse or pony that is too fat comes to stud, and has to be put on a restricted diet (because otherwise it may founder), it is likely to be more difficult to get into foal.

So, the mares should be well fed, but some will obviously need a lot more than others. A Thoroughbred mare with a foal at foot could easily require 8–11lb (4–5kg) of oats a day, as well as good pasture or hay.

Mares in very poor condition are not likely to get into foal, and their condition cannot be justified by saying, 'she puts everything into the foal at foot!'. Such a mare is simply not being fed enough good quality food for her needs.

Bad stud experience

Most mares like the company of stallions whether they are in season or not. If mares are allowed to wander loose, even if they are not in season they like to visit the stallions who are locked in yards. They enjoy having a good scream at the menfolk, with their tails madly swishing, loud snorts and squeals, and front legs slashing the air. Then they happily settle down to grazing nearby.

However, every now and then mares come to stud who are actually afraid of the stallion. If the stallion is a well-behaved horse and under restraint, there is no normal reason for this fear. In most cases, the mare has been taught to be afraid of the stallion. This may have happened by teasing the mare in a crush or some confined space where she felt trapped and frightened. She may have been hobbled and served without even being in season! Or the mare may have been served by an ill-behaved stallion who frightened or hurt her.

If the mare is frightened of the stallion, it is a good idea to keep her in a yard or paddock near the stallion, so that she can get to know and accept him without fear.

A bad experience at stud can condition a mare into suppressing outward signs of being in season when she actually is in oestrus.

Maiden mares

Maiden mares have an undeserved bad reputation, and some studs refuse to take them. However, an earlier bad stud experience should be one problem they don't have, and it is rare that the mare should refuse to accept the stallion when matters are managed properly. Nevertheless, although only a minute number of mares refuse to accept the stallion when they are properly teased and fully in oestrus; those that do reject him tend to be maiden mares.

Bint el Bellona was an Arabian mare that came to stud as a three-year-old. She was teased daily by the stallion, and after a week or two she came into season. 'Yes please!' she said to him. 'Yes, yes, yes!'

So the stallion was promptly led around behind her and stopped still, just out of range of her hind legs. Instead of giving him an even more enthusiastic come on, she said furiously, 'If you dare, I will kill you!'

Had we been too hasty? Had we not teased her enough? So the stallion was backed away, the teasing barrier which was only a mesh-covered cyclone gate was shut between them, and the stallion was asked to tease her over the gate again. 'Yes pleeease!' she said most enthusiastically.

We backed the stallion off a few yards. 'Don't go!' implored the mare with a great show of obscene body language. So we opened the gate between them, but once again the mare became a hate-filled fury!

Why was there such a dramatic difference in her behaviour when the cyclone gate was opened? She certainly wasn't afraid of the stallion. What was to be done?

'I'll give her a dose of prostaglandins when she goes out of season', said the vet. 'Then, when she comes back in she will stand.'

But she didn't.

'I will give her a dose of tranquilliser,' said the vet. 'Then she will stand for the stallion.'

But she didn't.

'We'll hobble her!' we said. And as we had never had to hobble a horse before, we had to make ourselves some makeshift hobbles out of dog collars and ropes, so that she couldn't massacre the stallion with her back legs.

We teased her again, and she said 'Yes!' again; and we opened the gate again, and she said 'No!' again. So we put the hobbles and a nose twitch on her, and a competent man held her, and the handler said 'Okay!' to the stallion.

Away we went! In spite of the restraints, she dragged

everyone fully twenty yards, and right into the middle of the manure heap! We all fell over: horses and people. Blackened heads, bodies, and legs protruded everywhere from the foul-smelling muck!

But we got our way. And the stallion had his way with her! And no doubt the manure heap was her revenge on us all!

Fortunately we didn't even have to think of serving her two days later, as she had gone out of season! She subsequently proved to be in foal, and eventually produced the best foal her owners had ever bred.

Not in the mood!

The mare may not say she has a headache! But there are frequent times that the mare may not be in the mood for the stallion – even if she is teased properly and at length. These times include when she may be expecting a dinner rather than being served up to the stallion instead! She may be worried about her foal. She may not like love in a cold climate, and rain may turn her off altogether. Most mares appear to be quite turned off the stallion on a rainy day, yet may have shown that they wanted him the day before when it was sunny and the day after the rain when it was fine again! The mare may also not 'show' to the stallion if she is very anxious, has been separated from her companions, or has already taken a fancy to another male horse.

Worry about her foal

It is only natural that a mare will worry about her foal and will not want to be separated from it. So although we don't have the foal running loose when the mare is served in case it is injured, we do restrain it nearby so that she can see that it is all right. An assistant may hold the foal; or the foal may be placed in a stable or a special small yard, and the mare can watch it over the stable door or the yard's rail top while she is being served.

Psychological problems of the stallion

Psychologists tell us that children play in a way that helps to prepare them for the realities of adulthood. This is also true of horses. Colt foals play in a way that prepares them for maturity. Unlike fillies, they play very rough games, standing on their hind legs biting each other: they are learning to fight as a stallion would. They play games with their mother too, and stand up on their hind legs with their front legs over her back, a skill they will need as a mature breeding stallion. The young colt, through play with others, prepares himself for a future role as herd protector and sire.

Inappropriate behaviour with mares due to isolation

Many colt foals do not have the opportunity to play with others. Even worse, they are frequently isolated from other horses so that their communication skills are limited. So when they are eventually presented with a mare to serve, they not only don't know what to do, but they behave inappropriately. They may show no interest at all; they may try and play with the mare; or they may even try and attack her.

The advantages of a horse being a paddock stallion are obvious enough; but there is the risk of the stallion being injured, and also the disadvantage of not knowing if and when mares are served.

So on most studs, stallions have their own separate quarters and hand serve the mares. Consequently it will be of great importance that a stallion's life has been, and continues to be, as close as possible to that of an ordinary horse; and he continues to have some normal contact with mares so that he will easily and successfully serve them. Otherwise, the chances are that he will be so overexcited when he is asked to cover a mare, that he will do everything wrong.

The stallion's territory (stable, yard, and paddock) should be arranged so that he can see some of the stud farm's own mares nearby, and he can talk to them nose to nose. This can be achieved with the use of appropriate double fencing between his yard and the mares' paddock, or weld mesh between his stable and that of neighbouring mares or foals. It is better for the stallion to have the same mares around him all the time as changes will tend to make him upset. Visiting mares, and all their comings and goings, are best kept further away, as stallions tend to be very conscious and sensitive to the slightest changes made around them.

Of course, the stallion's yard and stable should be exclusively his. It is lacking in tact, and most upsetting to the horse, to put another horse or stallion in his territory when he is elsewhere.

Inappropriate behaviour due to lack of exercise and obedience

The stallion should be exercised – and outside his own territory. An unexercised stallion tends to get overexcited if taken out of his own area, especially if he has been confined to a stable or yard. And if he is taken to serve a mare, he may become quite uncontrollable.

If the horse is not broken in, he is lunged every day for the sake of his physical fitness, for making him gentler and more manageable, and for reinforcing the idea of being obedient to his handler. If the colt or stallion is rather boisterous, we lunge him before serving a mare to let him dissipate some of his excess exuberance.

We prefer to exercise a stallion by riding him. It is fun

for both of us. Additionally, it not only helps to make the horse fit and healthy, but also greatly improves the horse's psychological well being by providing greater variety and interest in the day. Riding the stallion also enables a closer bond or partnership to form between the horse and person which will be of tremendous help in the difficult and risky business of serving mares.

The horse must be able to trust his handler

The horse needs to be able to trust his handler that he will not be kicked by the mare, especially as we insist that the stallion must be obedient to us and not follow his own inclinations. If a young stallion is kicked by a mare it could well condition him into refusing to serve mares in the future. If a more experienced stallion gets kicked, there is also the risk of psychological damage to the stallion so that serving mares properly becomes difficult and less likely. Of course, if any stallion is kicked hard enough it can be permanently physically damaged too.

Older stallions that have been properly managed in the serving of mares, learn through their own experience, and may become very clever at knowing if a mare will stand for them or not. So the wise handler also listens to what his horse is telling him.

Many people use hobbles to protect the stallion from being kicked; but there are also risks in using hobbles. Besides, those that use hobbles are all too easily tempted to serve mares when they are not properly in season. A mare that is not in season, if served, will not get into foal.

The mare that is in season will keep all four feet on the ground if she has been properly teased. She will not attempt to kick or strike the stallion. Only about one or two per cent of mares would be an exception to this rule; and even then, if the stallion handler is experienced the horse should come to no harm.

Using the young stallion

When we want to use a young stallion that has never served a mare before it is important that he is obedient and well-behaved; so that he can be taught to do his 'job' properly, and also learn the good manners that are expected of him.

For this purpose we use a mare who is fully in season and has a known record of obliging behaviour towards stallions. It is a help if she is also smaller than the stallion.

The stallion is led slowly up to the mare, who is on the other side of a teasing barrier, and is invited to tease her and sniff her from end to end.

When it appears that he is ready to serve, he should immediately be led around to the mare who is being held still by an assistant. The stallion should be walked up slowly behind the mare, but to the near side so that she can see him. The stallion is stopped short of the mare's hind legs so that the handler can doubly ascertain that the mare will continue to invite the stallion and that she will not lash out. The stallion is then asked to come close to the mare's near side, and then to move backwards into position to mount her. This is much safer for the stallion than mounting the mare directly from behind.

On no account must the stallion be allowed to mount the mare if he is not physically able to serve her. He will have to be teased up again to renew his interest. Neither should he be allowed to leap on the mare from a distance, nor be permitted to bite her.

We know when the stallion has actually succeeded in serving the mare because his tail 'flags' up and down, maybe once, maybe more. The stallion then will probably dismount, or can be encouraged to do so with a pull of the lead rope. At the same time, the assistant who is holding the mare should turn her head towards the stallion who is dismounting to the near side, so that if by any chance she should kick she will be angled so that it misses him and his handler.

The stallion needs to tease his own mares

The stallion should always tease the mares that he is going to serve. This makes sure that by the time the mare comes into season that the horses know each other and he will be more relaxed and she won't be frightened. If he teases his own mares it also prevents the possibility of her getting attached to another horse and refusing to be served by the stallion.

It is also a matter of tact never to tease or serve mares in front of other stallions.

Teasing mares is hard on a stallion and he needs lots of positive encouragement not to turn sour or nasty. So we always make sure that the last mare of the day to be teased will also be served by him as his reward.

Lack of basic physiological and behavioural knowledge

Another reason for the low percentage of mares at stud getting into foal is a lack of basic physiological and behavioural knowledge of mares by the stud master.

Although most mares come into 'season', or oestrus, for approximately five days every three weeks, some come into season for a shorter period – perhaps only a single day. So if a mare is not teased every day until she comes into season, she may be missed altogether.

Additionally, mares sometimes exhibit ambivalent behaviour towards the stallion. They seek his company and behave as if they are in season, but strike and kick at the same time. Mares that act like this are not in season, and may even be many months in foal. However, such ambivalent behaviour most frequently occurs before the mare is fully in oestrus and when she is going out. Sometimes this period of obviously mixed emotions when the mare is 'coming in' may last from one hour to several days. Mares exhibiting this behaviour are frequently and wrongly hobbled-up and served – and just as frequently they fail to get into foal from this service.

A mare that is fully in season will stand for the stallion without attempting to kick or strike him, providing that she has been properly teased beforehand. It is most unusual to come across a mare who genuinely needs to be hobbled to protect the stallion. Unfortunately for many mares, some people use hobbles as a substitute for knowledge, and serve the mare at a time when she will not conceive.

A mare is always served on the first day she comes into season, in case she is one of the few who is in season for only one day. Vets regard it as desirable to serve the mare once every second day until she goes out of season.

Overuse of the stallion reduces his fertility. The stallion should never be used more than three times a day, and then only occasionally and with the matings spaced as far apart as possible. Two matings a day or less is preferable, and only once a day for old or very young stallions.

Inadequate or incompetent teasing of mares

I usually only met 'David' once a year, and that was at the biggest Arabian horse show in the state. One year he was ecstatic. He had just imported into Australia from the USA an Arabian mare of Polish breeding to put to his Egyptian stallion. So it goes.

'And', he added to all this information, 'I've got this great way of teasing mares! I've built a sorta passageway so they can't get away from the stallion!'

I raised my eyebrows in amazement. 'But David . . .' I said. But being only a female I wasn't permitted to speak.

The Polish mare didn't get into foal that year, although she was hobbled and served numerous times.

The next year when I met David again he said, 'Ah! A real horseman has showed me how to tease the mares. Ya put a twitch on them and rope them, and what do ya know? Nearly all of them show they're in season after all!' Surprisingly for David, none of the mares got into foal after this treatment either.

Next year David was rather downcast. 'The only way to know when the mares are in season,' he said, 'is to get the vet to follicle test them; and I can't afford that!'

Nevertheless, David had been getting some foals each year, because he also had a paddock stallion that lived with a number of mares. But the Polish mare, like the other special mares she lived with in a paddock near the house, still failed to get into foal.

I dreaded meeting David at the show the following year, but he rang me on some business matter before it eventuated and asked would I come over.

He greeted me with great enthusiasm, and immediately hurried me down to the paddock to see – well I thought to see – a colt he had recently bought and had put in a makeshift yard he had hastily erected at one end of his special mares' paddock. But instead, he ignored the colt, and began jumping up and down in a frenzy of excitement, pointing to the bare ground outside the colt's fence.

'I've found it! I've found it!' he shouted, and in puzzlement I looked at the dark damp patches in the pale grey dirt, where mares in season had come up during the night to visit the colt, and had urinated their come hither invitation to him.

'They're in season! They're in season!' David exclaimed joyously. 'Now all I have to do is to work out which ones!' So it goes.

Frequently, mares that are in season do not openly display the fact as obviously as described in horse-breeding books, and as a consequence stud masters often misconstrue a mare's behaviour. Additionally, if a mare is hurt or frightened when she is teased by the stallion she may give a false answer. She may appear to say 'yes' and urinate out of fear rather than as an invitation to the stallion. Hence the folly of nose-twitching a mare, teasing in a crush or other restricted space, or using an ill-behaved stallion.

The mare should be teased properly each day until she comes into season, and should be teased until she says 'yes' or 'no' to the stallion. Kicking, striking, or the more subtle responses of ears back or tail swishing, may all designate 'no' answers.

Some mares will give an immediate and valid 'yes' or 'no' response: whilst others may have to be teased for longer. Some mares may start off being rather unenthusiastic about the stallion, and then may warm up and say 'yes'. Teasing should not take longer than necessary as it is unfair to both horses.

Most mares prefer a stallion who is patient and gentle, sniffing them from end to end; rather than a noisy, over keen, under-disciplined horse who frightens them and tries to leap on them without even a polite 'hullo' first.

Instead of upsetting the mares by bringing them in to be teased, we lead the stallion past the mares' paddocks each day, and watch the response of the mares. Usually those that are nowhere near to coming into season give him a bored look and then go on eating; although some mares who are not in season like to come up and say 'hullo', and slash the air with their front legs just to tell him that he is not really wanted! We tease the mares, or let the mares tease themselves, over the farm gates which are suitably covered with a strong mesh that the horses can't kick a leg through. Of course, we couldn't do this with an ill-mannered stallion, because he would not only frighten the shy mares away, but he would also be likely to try and throw himself over the top of the gate to get at the mares and so injure himself in the process.

Most of the mares that are in season will make their desire for the stallion quite obvious without having to catch and actively tease them, and any mares for which there is a possibility of them coming into season who have not teased themselves are caught and conveniently teased over the gate.

We don't take the stallion into the paddock because there is the danger of him being attacked by a jealous mare. A mare may be possessive of another mare, and may attempt to attack the stallion to keep him away from her!

If a mare needs to be served, she is brought in at the end of the teasing session. Her tail is bandaged; she is teased again; and then covered by the stallion. The mare is then returned to her paddock, as any changes in her environment may make her less likely to conceive.

The mares that come to stud all have different personalities and different experience, and consequently may only show that they are in season in completely different circumstances.

Most mares that are in season or oestrus will 'show' to the stallion if they are quietly led up to him when he is behind the safety of a farm gate or stable door. Some mares will only show to the stallion if hand teased in this way. These mares are often older horses who have been conditioned to this behaviour by earlier stud experience. Such mares in the paddock with a paddock stallion may never be served.

However, some mares behave in the reverse fashion. They will only show to be in season if they are turned loose and allowed to approach the stallion when they feel like it.

Many mares will not show that they are in season, even with extensive teasing, if they have something else on their mind. For example:

- A mare that has just arrived at stud may be too worried and anxious to show to a stallion even if she is in season
- A mare that is expecting her dinner may have no interest in the stallion until after she has eaten

- A mare may not show to a stallion if she has already taken a fancy to another stallion or gelding, especially one of a different colour to the stallion
- A mare may be quite uninterested in the stallion during bad weather, such as if it is cold and raining
- A mare that is worried about her foal may not show, and may be particularly aggressive towards the stallion.

Some studs like to use a teaser, which is rather cruel to the horse, and can also be a disadvantage as many mares will not accept a change in horse when it is time to be served. Teasers, geldings, and other stallions are best kept away from the mare, so that she does not become attached to them to the exclusion of the serving stallion.

Veterinary assistance

If a mare exhibits signs of illness, or infection, or has a history that could indicate a breeding problem, a veterinary examination may be necessary. However, veterinary assistance may also be required for the prospective brood mare who is in good health but does not exhibit normal reproductive activity. As a guide, the services of a vet are required:

- If the mare fails to come into season after four weeks of competent teasing
- If the mare fails to go out of season after a reasonable time, say ten days
- If the mare fails to conceive after she has been through two cycles and has been served adequately each time
- To perform a forty-two day pregnancy test on a mare who has been served and has not come back into season; to determine whether the mare is in foal or not, and if not to give appropriate treatment.

It is not very difficult to beat the odds, to be more successful than the national average in breeding horses; and, unless we are unlucky, we should be able to do better than Old Mother Nature herself!

10

GIVE YOUR HORSE A BREAK!

To many people the idea of breaking in their own horse would seem to be unwise, if not foolish. The thought conjures up visions of plunging and bucking horses, and the necessity for great strength and bravery. Nothing need be further from the truth.

We can teach horses to do what we want through our understanding of them; not by using force or pain. We can break in a horse without it wanting to throw us off; if we avoid making the horse anxious, frightened, or angry. We can educate a horse without it wanting to resist us; if we avoid confrontations with the horse. Instead, we motivate the horse with positive rewards to do what we want.

There are a number of advantages in breaking in our own horse. The greatest advantage of course is the sheer pleasure of creating our own horse. However, there is another consideration. At the present time horsebreakers are unlicensed, unregistered, and often untrained, unskilled, and unkind. Anyone can claim to break in horses; and if they create problems in our horse, or even turn our horse into a nervous or physical wreck, it seems that there is very little that we can do about it.

There's an additional problem, too, in sending our horse to a horsebreaker: it's us! We may not have prepared the horse sufficiently well for its breaking in to be as successful as possible. We may expect the horsebreaker to make up for our own insufficient handling of the horse in its earlier years. We may expect the horse we can't catch to become friendly; the horse we can't halter to be easy to handle; feet that have never been picked up to be easy to shoe; and the horse that is rarely caressed or disciplined to become a calm and confident riding horse. Such fairy tales rarely come true. No horsebreaker can rectify the deficiencies of years in a few weeks.

Irrespective of how capable and competent the horsebreaker, the horse cannot accept a lot of learning in a short period of time without becoming anxious or distressed. This anxiety will show in behavioural problems, like being hard to catch, distrust of people, nervousness, tongue over the bit, crossing its jaws, rearing, erratic paces, and so on.

There's also another problem in not beginning a horse's training until it is mature: its temperament.

'No worries!' we may say. 'My Beautiful has such a marvellous temperament . . . He'll only require a few weeks work!'

Many people are convinced that their horse has a marvellous temperament because it is always very happy to accept loads of food, titbits, and caresses from them. 'He's a real sweetheart!' they say. However, it is not easy to know if an untrained horse has a good temperament until we try and teach it something. A horse with a good temperament is willing to learn. However, we may not realise that our horse has a poor temperament until we try to break it in and we find it is quite uncooperative.

If we send our horse to someone else to break in we may

feel that any unwillingness will be cured; but unfortunately that does not necessarily happen. A stubborn horse that is 'broken in' can still argue with us every step of the way. It may be simply an every day tussle, year in year out, of the horse always trying to do something different from what we are asking of it. Or it may be so difficult and unmanageable that only a few of the most experienced riders can cope with it.

The best way to teach an unwilling horse new things, is to teach it all the basics as a foal, so that very early in its life it forms a habit and expectation of doing what *we* want, before it gets too set in its own ways. Then as an older horse it will be more obliging than it otherwise would have been.

So whether the horse is going to be broken in by a horsebreaker or by us, it is essential that the basic training of the horse is learnt *before* the official breaking in period starts.

The horse should be calm and relaxed about being touched all over by a person; and it should accept being held still, led, tied-up, rugged, and having its feet picked up and handled. In other words, if the horse is to be broken in successfully, we will have to do a lot of work beforehand anyway!

Additionally, the horse that learns these basic skills when it is a foal not only learns them better, but should be easy to break in when mature because most of the work is already done!

If we have an affinity for horses, and if our riding skills have had professional polishing, such a task can only be a pleasure.

Handling foals

It is of considerable advantage to us if a horse starts to learn some basic skills from the day it is born. This not only makes the horse easy to manage from the very beginning, but also gives us the very real pleasure of handling a trusting and friendly foal.

The first three days

The first three days of a foal's life are especially important, not only from the physical point of view, but also because they will greatly influence our future relationship with the horse.

A newborn foal normally accepts all that is around it. However, once it is more than three days old it is considerably more cautious or suspicious about anything that is new or different, which may include us if we have not been handling it. So we need to take this opportunity of handling the foal in its first three days in the world when it is easy to do so. Otherwise, we may find that when the foal is only a few days older it will not let us touch it.

Teaching the foal to like being touched

We should begin handling the foal on the first day it is born. We don't worry and disturb the mare with an excessive amount of our presence, but each time we check the mare or foal for some physical reason we stroke and talk quietly to the foal too.

Many books have been written on the health of foal and mare at this stage of their lives, so only a little will be said here.

After the birth of the foal we check that both the mare and foal are all right. The stump of the navel cord of the newborn foal is soaked in some suitable disinfectant like tincture of iodine as soon as possible. The mare is given a feed and we check that she has a good supply of fresh water. We watch that the placenta or afterbirth has been passed, and if it hasn't within eight hours we notify the vet. We make sure that the foal has learnt to drink within four or five hours, and if it hasn't we will have to help it to nurse. We also watch for the passing of the meconium, the faecal matter that is in the digestive tract of the foal when it is born, and if it is not passed the foal may be constipated and need veterinary assistance.

It is just as well to have the vet check over the mare and foal within the first twenty-four hours of the foal's birth, and have him or her give the foal some routine post-natal preventative medicine in the form of antibiotics and tetanus antitoxin. Antibiotics and treatment of the navel cord dramatically reduce the chances of the newborn foal getting navel ill and other serious infections.

So each time we perform the physical requirements for the mare or foal we also stroke and talk to the foal. We approach the foal slowly, and in as non-threatening a way as possible. We talk quietly, and bend low to make ourselves seem smaller and less intimidating. We stroke the foal's neck and body with our hands. We don't pat it! Neither do we try and touch its head or face until it is more used to us, as our hand coming towards its eyes would instinctively frighten it.

We stroke the foal, and caress the foal, and gradually it learns not only to accept being touched but also to enjoy being caressed. It begins to like us and to trust us.

Holding the foal

Also on the first day we can hold the foal two or three times. We hold the foal still, with our arms wrapped around it – one arm around its chest and the other around its hindquarters. It is its first lesson in discipline and accepting our authority. It will protest. The first time we try holding the foal it will probably attempt to rear and plunge, perhaps stomp on our toes or kick us in the shins. Nevertheless, we hold on. It's character forming – for both of us! We hold it and caress it, and then when it is standing quietly, we don't just let it go, but *we back off from it.* We leave it: so it doesn't learn the idea of leaving us!

The next day when we hold it again, the foal will be better behaved. Gradually it will accept out restraint and even be reassured by our presence. However, if we had made the mistake of letting the foal escape the first time we tried to hold it, we would find that the next time it would be harder to catch as it would have learnt the idea of running away from us. We cannot afford to make mistakes with young horses as they will learn the opposite of what we intend!

There is also another advantage in the foal learning to stand still in our arms. It learns to accept the sight of us above it, which will be of great advantage when it is first mounted and ridden (as a mature horse) as it will already be used to seeing a person above it.

Additionally, a foal that is used to being handled and held, will be much easier to treat if any illness or injury should happen to it.

Learning to lead

We like to stable mares and their newborn foals overnight and to take them out to the paddock each day. So rather than having the foal running loose and sometimes wandering off in another direction, we teach the foals to lead. Besides, it is really easy to teach them to lead when they are very young.

The foal has learnt to accept us holding it in our arms, and so does not require much more teaching to learn to lead. An assistant leads the mare and we follow with the foal. We hold the foal, but this time we push it along with our arm which is behind it; and instead of our other arm around its chest we have a soft towel around its neck so that it is easier for us to walk. The foal soon gets the idea and after a few days doesn't require many encouraging pushes from behind.

Learning to balance and accept the feet being picked up

Once the foal is used to being held and stroked all over, it is time to start picking up its feet. If we do not have someone to help us, the first few times we try doing this the foal is likely to lose its balance and walk off. So, to prevent it from getting upset and resisting us picking up its feet in the future, it is a good idea to have someone to help us in the beginning.

We make sure that the foal's feet are in a balanced position under it, and then while one person holds the foal in their arms on one side of it the second person on the other side can gently stroke a leg and then pick it up; but only for a few seconds the first couple of times. Then the same procedure can be followed for the two legs on the other side. After a while the second person won't be needed.

This good habit of allowing its feet to be picked up needs to be continually reinforced for the next few years. We find it a good idea when we feed the horses each evening to pick up their feet while their heads are glued to the feed bucket and they are not motivated to move away. The value of doing this will be obvious to anyone who has ever tried picking up the feet of a mature horse who has never had his legs handled before!

Acceptance of the headstall

By now the foal has learnt to accept and enjoy being stroked all over with our hands, and being scratched with our fingertips. So we can start putting its headstall on and off each day. This is easy enough with most well-handled foals. We do not leave the headstall on because of the danger of it being caught on something.

If the foal is not as cooperative as we would like, we find it easiest to put the headstall on in a corner of the stable with the foal positioned so that it cannot run backwards – we can use our arm to stop it from running forwards. There are two ways to do it. We can put an arm over the horse's neck and hold the noseband open with both our hands and gently and slowly put it on. If the foal takes fright and tries to leap forward, it can't because our arms and headstall make a loop against its chest and prevent it. The second method of headstalling is usually more successful. Both straps on the headstall are undone. Then the one that goes behind the horse's ears is done up lower down than usual and around the horse's neck. It is then gently brought up to a slightly more normal position, and then the second strap around the nose is carefully fastened. After a few days the horse will accept the headstall coming off and on in a more conventional manner.

Talking to horses

Whenever we handle a horse we talk to it. Horses are very sensitive to noise, so we keep our voice soft and quiet to soothe and reassure the horse. It doesn't matter what we say: it's all in the tone of the voice. Loud, excited, or angry voices can disturb and even frighten a horse; and yelling at a horse is for some a severe reprimand.

Unacceptable behaviour in foals

Sometimes foals like to bite, especially if they are colts. Biting is part of their play behaviour with each other. So if one bites us and we smack it, we are joining in the game and it may try to bite us again. However, this time, because the foal expects another smack, he immediately throws his head up in the air; and there is the beginning of another problem, the horse that is difficult to halter or bridle.

The only real solution is to learn to anticipate horses' actions and not to get bitten. All too frequently people feed themselves to a horse. They stroke and fiddle with the horse's mouth and lips, and then complain when the horse responds and bites them.

Another problem may be the foal that unexpectedly kicks us, and if we are fast enough to kick it back (on some nice muscley part like its rump where it won't do any harm) before it is out of reach, it will probably learn enough respect for people not to try such a stunt again. However, we must catch it soon afterwards and give it a scratch and cuddle so that it continues to like us and does not learn to fear us – only to respect us.

However, another foal may have a general style of ill behaviour towards us. When we walk in the paddock the foal may gallop up to us and rear in our face, or go cavorting past and kick us in the shins, and be gone before we can react. Usually properly handled foals do not behave like this. Most likely the foal has been touched but not held, or stroked but not taught to lead. It has learnt familiarity, but not respect. We have to teach the foal to respect us, as well as to like us. If it does not respect us we are in for a lot of trouble, and if it does not like us it will be harder to handle and more difficult to motivate to do what we want.

If we ignore the foal's unacceptable behaviour he could become increasingly dangerous as he gets older, stronger, and larger. We cannot punish the foal, because punishment must be instantaneous; and this foal is already out of our reach. The problem is best solved by teaching the horse something new. If we go about teaching him to lead properly he will learn to respect us and should continue to like and trust us.

Learning to lead in a halter

For the foal that has learnt to lead in the simple manner described for the newborn foal, with an arm behind and a towel around its neck, progression to leading with a headstall and rope is very simple. The foal is already accustomed to having the headstall put on, and a lead rope is attached. The foal may need to be prompted to move forward by being occasionally touched on the rump, which will remind it of its earlier lessons. The foal is always led next to the person, and should not be encouraged to follow. We don't want to teach the horse something that has to be unlearnt later.

Grooming the foal

Initially we groom the foal with our hands. It learns to accept us stroking it, and our fingertips scratching behind its ears, in its armpits, on itchy spots, and at chunks of dirt stuck on its sides. It can also learn to accept being brushed all over with a soft brush, and curry-combed if it has a long coat. We need to use the grooming tools very carefully, and only a soft brush should be used over bones.

Weanlings

Foals are usually weaned at about five or six months of age. Less than four months of age is too stressful for the foal. Later than six months is unnecessarily physically draining on the mare, especially if she is in foal again.

Foals are most successfully weaned if they have companions and they are already used to eating hay and a few pounds of grain each day. Foals are weaned together; two who are friends share a stable; or a larger number can share a safe yard, preferably one with a high chain-link or weld-mesh fence that feet can't be caught in or kick through. If we are going to wean a single foal, it needs to be friendly with and accustomed to being with another horse before it is actually weaned – perhaps a good-natured maiden mare or a gentle gelding who would be happy to be a babysitter.

The foals' mothers are usually taken out of sight and sound of their offspring, and are distracted from thinking too much about their foals by putting them in a paddock with other horses they are already familiar with. They them seem to miss their foals less.

However, sometimes a mare is very stressed at being parted from her foal, or the foal itself is over-stressed. If the anxiety of separation causes either horse to sweat, or to continually run around or call, it may be better not to totally separate mare and foal. It is only necessary to stop the foal nursing on the mare. Foals can be weaned very successfully just by separating them with a good mesh fence. Neither horse may have a real need to be with the other: they may be happy just to *see* that the other is all right.

Now that the mare and foal are separated, the foal will need to be given a substantial amount of grain and alfalfa hay each day. Whereas the mare, because we want to stop her milk production and dry her off, will only be given meadow hay for several days. The mare has been used to being well fed, she expects to be fed; so even if there is good grass in her paddock we give her some meadow hay, so that she doesn't feel totally forgotten and become stressed from that cause as well.

If the mare is distressed some twelve hours after separating her from her foal because her udder has become very full and painful, it is a good idea to milk out some of the milk to relieve the pressure. A second reduction of milk another twenty-four hours later is only occasionally necessary, and after this time the mare should dry off without any further trouble.

If the foals are stabled to wean them, it is particularly important to handle them and take them for a walk outside each day, as stabling can make them very anxious and quite unmanageable.

Teaching older foals to lead

Teaching older foals to lead can be difficult. Presuming that the foal is quite untame, we must first make friends with it. If the foal is in a yard with its mother or other foals, we can go and sit on the ground (to be as unthreatening as possible) and leave it to the foal's natural curiousity to make it come and investigate us. Gradually the foal will become used to our presence and we will be able to start stroking the foal's chest and body. When the foal gets more used to us we can stand up very slowly and caress more of the foal. Then, if the foal is not too big, and we are strong enough, we can put our arms around the foal and hold it, as with the newborn foal. However, we must not make a mistake and let it go before it will stand quietly. It will take several days, at least, to teach the foal to accept us.

Older foals are unlikely to learn to lead as easily as very young foals, and if possible it is a good idea if it can have its first leading lesson in the confined space of a stable.

A headstall is put on the foal, and a lead rope is attached. The weight of the lead rope alone is enough to make some foals go completely demented, and to throw themselves up in the air and over backwards. We want to avoid such behaviour because the foal could break its neck or suffer brain damage. So we have to play the foal like a fish on a line, and know when we can take on the rope, and when we have to give totally, so that the foal doesn't succeed in throwing itself and injuring itself.

Once the foal learns in the stable to accept the headstall and lead rope without too much anxiety, we then introduce it to the rump rope; otherwise we would not be able to cope with the foal because of its size and strength.

The rump rope is a length of soft rope with a large loop at one end which goes around the horse's rump above the hocks, and the other end of the rope is held in the opposite hand to the lead rope. The rump rope is pulled to encourage the horse to walk forwards and also held to stop it leaping backwards; while the lead rope also encourages the horse to walk forwards, but prevents it from leaping ahead.

The horse is then given a leading lesson or two in the stable before trying the great outdoors. If the foal has not yet been weaned it will be a great help to have someone lead the mare around for the foal to follow. Short lessons are best, so that the foal doesn't get cross and sour. Additionally, it is always best to end a lesson when things are going well, and not when they have gone wrong.

Teaching big weanlings to lead

Perhaps we have a really big and wild foal or weanling. We may be able to win its trust with food, as well as with caresses and scratching but putting the headstall on could be very difficult.

In this case we may be able to use a large and quiet horse as a moveable wall to block the foal in a corner of the stable while we quietly and gently put on the headstall. Nevertheless, it could be dangerous for us to try and teach a large foal to lead in a stable; and if we take it outside we could lose control.

So we attach a lead rope that is about three feet long to the headstall. The foal will stand on the rope every now and then, and so teach itself about the action of lead ropes. The rope should not be longer because we don't want it to wrap itself around the horse's legs and injure him. The foal will learn in a day or so not to throw itself backwards when we pull on the rope, and we will then be able to teach it to lead. This foal will also need the help of a rump rope.

Needless to say, there is every advantage in teaching a horse to lead in its first month of life. After that time, the disadvantages rapidly increase with the increasing age and size of the foal.

It is particularly important that colts are taught to lead properly before they become too strong, so that they will be obedient as stallions. The horse must believe that we are stronger than it! If a colt learns that he does not have to lead properly, we may have created a stallion that no one can fully control – especially when it comes to hand serving mares. The use of rearing bits and chains is not the answer. The more force that is used to control the horse in the first place, the more force will have to be continued to be used to control the horse.

Some people teach colts to lead in a chain or bit, instead of teaching a horse to lead properly in a headstall with a lead rope. Consequently, the horse has to always wear a chain or bit to be taken anywhere; and when it comes to serving a mare, a situation in which a stallion is highly motivated to do what he wants without listening to us, the stallion may be impossible to hold in check.

Learning to tie up

We teach the foal to lead before it is taught to tie up, so it understands the pull of the rope on the headstall and is less likely to try and break free or injure itself. A successful old horseman's strategy in teaching young horses to tie up, is to tie them to a car tyre's inner tube, that has been fastened about five feet above the ground in some safe place like a stable wall. The rubber of the inner-tube acts as a spring, and if the horse does pull back, there is less jolt and less panic.

Once the horse has learnt to tie up we may want to trailer it somewhere. When we trailer a horse for the first few times, especially youngsters, we put a rump rope on them too and fasten it to the breast bar. The rump rope prevents the horse pulling back and gaining enough space to then be able to leap forwards on to or over the breast bar.

Worming

All foals are wormed shortly after they are weaned unless they have already been started on a worming programme. It is very important how we go about worming a horse, because if we frighten the horse, or make it angry, it will be very difficult to worm in the future. And the future, as far as worming programmes are concerned, occurs at least every eight to twelve weeks, or over one hundred times in a horse's lifetime! Besides, horses hate being wormed because they dislike the taste of the stuff.

These days horses are most frequently wormed with commercial horse pastes packaged in disposable syringes. We find the simplest way to worm horses is as follows: we put a headstall and lead rope on the horse, stroke it and reassure it, and then quietly take hold of the horse's noseband – letting the lead rope drop on to the ground and standing on it with a foot instead. We then insert our thumb into the horse's mouth between the teeth and the cheek, and when the horse opens its mouth we squirt in the paste with our other hand. The horse is offended. Yuk! So we don't let it go immediately. We give it a bit of a scratch and a cuddle first. We have to undo the negative aspects of worming as much as possible.

Yearlings

Rugging

By the time a horse is one year old we are probably thinking of blanketing it against the winter's cold: horses usually need to be blanketed in cold or wet weather. If the horse is used to being stroked and groomed all over there should be no trouble in it accepting a blanket. But it may be just as well not to start blankcting it on a windy day!

We halter the horse, then show it the blanket and let it sniff it and see that it is not too terrible. Then we give the horse a handful of oats or some other titbits, and further reassure it by talking to it, and be standing right next to it so that our arm or body is in contact with its neck. Then keeping the blanket low, and without flapping it up into the air, we carefully and slowly put it over the horse's wither and spread it out. Meanwhile we are soothingly telling the horse how clever it is! If the horse is apprehensive, we continue giving it titbits until it relaxes. We then take it for a walk, and reassure it if it gets fussed by the sound and feel of the blanket on its back. Finally, when we release the horse, we do so in a situation where it will peacefully graze or eat hay, rather than run about.

Horses that have never been made anxious or frightened by their early blanketing experience, continue to accept blanketing and unblanketing in the open paddock without having to be haltered.

Lunging

We don't normally lunge yearlings, but occasionally it helps us to assess a horse's temperament. When we lunge a horse for the first time we get a very good indication of how willing the horse is and how amenable it will be to being broken in.

The horse is lunged out in the open in an unfenced area of flat land. Horses that put up so much resistance that two people are necessary to lunge it and prevent it from disappearing into the Never Never, prove to be the horses that are the most obstinate or difficult to train as riding horses.

When we lunge horses, we always lunge them in both directions so that their muscular development on both sides of their body is balanced and equal. Young horses can only be lunged for a few minutes each way because of the strain on their leg joints. They should also be lunged on a large circle for the same reason.

Breaking in

Breaking in a horse should be a happy time for the horse as well as ourselves. To achieve this we create the right circumstances for the horse to do what we want it to do naturally, and without causing any stress or conflict to either of us. We then reward the horse so that it will be happy to do the same thing again. The repetition of correct behaviour or movement then establishes it as a good habit. It also helps to teach the horse a habit of obedience in relation to us.

There are a few simple rules for breaking in a horse so that it is a pleasure for both of us. We avoid causing our horse anxiety. We communicate clearly to the horse and also listen to it. We motivate the horse with positive rewards. We don't overwork it, ask too much of it, or make it sour or bored; and if the novice horse does do something wrong, it is probably our mistake and we do not punish it.

Of course the horse may be a little anxious, but we must avoid making the horse so anxious that it resists or ignores us. If we make it frightened, excited, or angry, it may take no notice of us; worse, it may explode in an excess of emotion and learn to buck or rear or produce some other undesirable behaviour instead.

Training the horse should be a logical progression from one thing to the next; and although we expect the horse to learn something new each day, it may only be a very little. The steps are small and related, to avoid raising the horse's anxiety; and we do not progress to the next stage until the horse is relaxed and at ease with what it is already being taught.

We need good communication with the horse. Although the handler's or rider's demands of the horse must be quite clear so that the horse can have no doubt what is required of it, there is more to communication than just that.

Communicating well with a horse, being empathic with it, saves things going wrong. Of course we want to be able to ask a horse to do things; but being empathic with the horse can save us from the pitfalls of asking at the wrong time. If we are in rapport with the horse we will 'know' if it will accept and do what we ask. If it accepts our requests, we have gained; if it does not, and it resists, or becomes angry or anxious, we've lost ground in our training.

Short training sessions are best so that the horse doesn't become sour; and we always reward the horse at the end of its training session and give it a feed as soon as it has cooled down.

There are a considerable number of advantages in breaking in a horse with kindness and without causing it anxiety or stress. There is less physical and mental strain on us. The horse will not be motivated to resist us, so it should not learn any undesirable behaviour. The horse's self-esteem is not damaged, and may actually be enhanced. The horse's breaking in can be interrupted at any time without it regressing; as its training has been free of anxiety, it is not associated with anxiety, and so its resumption does not cause anxiety. Even stallions can be turned out for a long time, with the expectation of them being well-behaved when brought in. And horses continue to feel affection for us and remain happy to be caught. Some horses even feel deprived if they miss out on their daily ride and attention.

We find that horses that have been properly handled as youngsters, normally become pleasurable and proficient riding mounts within three or four weeks when we break them in as three-year-olds.

Preparations

Grooming

The horse is *always* groomed before its daily training, even if it appears clean. Grooming the horse before its training session helps to establish a mutual feeling of trust and ease between the horse and person. Grooming is also necessary for the health of the horse's skin and to make sure no lumps, grit, or prickles will be caught underneath the horse's gear. We double check the horse's skin in the saddle and girth areas with our hands and fingertips.

If the horse has not been handled very much as a foal, and therefore is not used to seeing people *above* it, we stand on a bale of hay to groom the horse. The horse needs to learn to accept us in this unexpected position, so that it doesn't take fright when we eventually sit up on its back.

We also pick out the horse's hooves each day to make sure no stones are wedged in them.

Leading from both sides

The horse has been taught to lead, but we now want to make sure that it will lead from both sides as that will make it easier to teach it to lunge in both directions.

Shoeing

The horse should have learnt to accept having its feet picked up and filed. It will now need to be shod as lunging and riding will wear its hooves.

Rugging

The horse is already used to being rugged. If it is not, we rug it now. If the weather is hot we only rug it at night when it is cool. Rugging and unrugging each day is a good preparation for saddling.

We begin

This programme is set out in days, but only as a guide or indication of progress. It is *not* a regimen to which we must adhere.

Day one

Lunging

The horse is taught to lunge for many reasons: to teach the horse obedience; to make the horse stronger and fitter; to teach the horse to balance itself and to flex both ways rather than just move in a straight line; to teach the horse the verbal commands 'trot!' and 'whoa!'; and later, when the horse starts work in a bridle and side-reins, to commence creating a good mouth on the horse. We use the principles of training and riding horses as described by Alois Podhajsky[32], and do not use the traditional and cruel 'horsemen's mouthing gear'.

A cavesson should be used when lunging the horse. If a leather headstall is used instead, it must be fitted very carefully, so that the weight or pull of the lunge rope when clipped to one side doesn't pull the headstall strap on the far side into the horse's eye. Additionally, it must also be adjusted so that it doesn't interfere with the horse's bit when it is later bridled.

The horse is groomed first of all, and then taken to the lunging area. We like to lunge and work the horse in an open area rather than a yard. It's more pleasant for both of us! The horse is taught to lunge to the left first, in an anti-clockwise direction, as horses seem to find it easier. We lead the horse around the circle a couple of times to give it the idea, and then back off giving it rope. We then encourage the horse to trot around the circle by 'popping' the lunge whip behind it.

The horse must not be frightened. So we talk to it in a quiet and relaxed way; and if it's very excited we try and impart a feeling of ease or even boredom to quieten it down. If the horse is afraid of the lunge whip we leave it on the ground until the horse is more confident.

The horse is only lunged for two or three minutes at the most on each side on the first day. We endeavour to get the horse to trot properly in a relaxed manner on a large circle. We do not want the horse just to run around in a circle; it will benefit very little. The handler keeps himself behind the movement of the horse so that he can encourage it forward if necessary from behind. He does not get ahead of the movement of the horse because he would then be leading the horse on the lunge rope; and as a consequence the horse would not carry itself properly with its hocks under it.

Horses that are very anxious or unwilling can be difficult to teach to lunge. The handler will need to use both hands on the lunge rope, so an assistant will be necessary to hold the lunging whip and prevent the horse from doubling backwards.

We teach the horse while it is on the lunge the verbal

commands of 'trot!' and 'whoa!'. It may take the horse a number of days to learn them. Each time we want the horse to trot we give it the verbal command and pop the whip behind it. The horse soon gets the right idea. 'Whoa!' is more difficult.

The horse is trotting and we want it to stop, so we ask it to 'whoa!'. Unsurprisingly the horse ignores us because it does not know what we mean. So we ask the horse to stop on the circle with a repeated 'taking' action of the lunge as well as with the verbal command 'whoa!'. We may even have to move out to the circle ourselves, shortening the rope, and as we take hold of the horse to stop it we continue to repeat the command 'whoa!'. We move out to the horse rather than bring it in to us, because if the horse learns to come in to us it will eventually do so whenever it feels like ending the lunging session. This is a most annoying habit and can be hard to cure.

Even if we think the horse did less well than we expected, it is still rewarded and stroked and given some titbit for good measure – or more precisely, so that it will be happy to be lunged again. Additionally, the horse is always given a feed before it is turned loose at the end of its training session.

The next day the horse should lunge more easily and in a more relaxed fashion; and it will understand better what we want it to do. So we lunge it for four minutes on each side.

The horse is always rewarded when it is being broken in, and most other times too. The reward not only motivates the horse to do what we want, but reassures the horse that we aren't trying to be mean to it!

On the third day the horse can be lunged for five minutes on each side, and by the fourth day the horse is usually relaxed and confident about lunging so we can then progress to saddling.

The horse is never lunged for more than five minutes a

side, unless it is a very obstreperous colt and then ten minutes is the upper limit. If the horse is not amenable after this period of time we are doing something very wrong!

Day 4

Saddling

The horse is groomed all over as usual, paying particular attention to the girth area with our fingertips. We show the saddlecloth and the saddle to the horse, reassure it, give it a handful of a favourite food like a horse mix, and put the gear gently on the horse's back. The horse is continually reassured with quiet talk, handfuls of grain, and stroking of the neck. The girth is done up very loosely and is gradually tightened one hole at the time on alternate sides. After each tightening the handler's fingers are run between the girth and the horse to make sure no skin or hair has been caught. It also gets the horse used to more contact in this area. The girth is tightened until it is tight enough to hold the saddle in place but not tight enough to mount. On no account is the horse to be made anxious. More time may be needed for it to accept the tightness of the girth without being upset. If so, it can be given some alfalfa hay to eat or be allowed to browse on the grass while someone holds it for ten minutes or so before the girth is tightened again.

The horse should then be lunged the usual five minutes on each side. The horse may be a little worried when it first starts trotting and feels the saddle bumping on its back, but should relax in the first half minute or so. If we have been handling the horse properly it is most unlikely to buck or misbehave. We are concerned that the horse doesn't buck or misbehave, because we don't want it to even think of such behaviour in relation to saddles or being ridden – otherwise we may have just taught it a bad habit.

Day 5

Further tightening of the girth

The horse is saddled in the same fashion, and the girth is tightened one hole at the time. This time the horse's girth can probably be tightened sufficiently to support a mounting rider, which possibly will be only one hole tighter than the previous day. The girth should be no tighter than is necessary to hold the saddle in place. It is important that the horse is not worried by the girth, and if the handler continues to be considerate about doing it up it is likely that the horse will never learn the annoying habit of blowing itself up.

The horse is then lunged the usual five minutes each side.

The horse is accustomed to stirrups and noise in the saddle

After the horse has been lunged the stirrups are lowered and the horse is led about with them dangling. Then, when the horse is relaxed about that, the handler halts the horse and bangs the saddle with the flat of his hand in such a way that it will accustom the horse to sounds coming from the saddle but without frightening it.

Weight on the stirrups

It is of great importance that the horse will accept our full weight in the near side stirrup before it is actually mounted. It is in the moment of mounting, before we have actually arrived in the saddle, that we are most vulnerable to any misbehaviour or sudden movement by the horse. It is not the weight that upsets the horse, but the drag on its girth; and the consequent fright could make it buck or leap forward – unacceptable behaviour which we do not want to initiate.

So, to teach the horse to accept our weight in the stirrup we reassure the horse, then take hold of the stirrup leather as high up as possible with both hands and gradually put more and more weight on it until our feet are completely off the ground. We stop immediately if the horse starts getting upset. We may not be able to put our full weight on the stirrup leather until we have done it a number of times, and some horses may require several days to accept it. We continue hanging our weight on the stirrup leather on both sides until the horse is perfectly at ease. We will then be able to mount the horse via the stirrup.

Day 6

Bridling

Although each day is a progression, with the horse learning a little more; we also go back to the beginning each day and work through what has been learnt to consolidate it and help keep the horse confident and relaxed.

We can now begin to bridle the horse. We like to use a smooth, unjointed, stainless-steel, snaffle bit because it is softer on the horse's mouth, and because, being unjointed, it is harder for the horse to get its tongue over it if the horse is so inclined. The horse can graduate to a jointed snaffle at a later stage if we feel that it is desirable.

We put on the bridle, one without reins, very carefully and gently: we encourage the horse to accept the bit with a handful of oats, and we are especially careful not to hurt the horse's ears. Horses usually play with the bit for a few minutes, and then just accept it. The horse is then saddled, and lunged, and so on. (The lunge rope continues to be attached to the cavesson or headstall. It is never attached to the bridle.) The bridle is removed at the end of the training session.

Day 7

Side-reins

We can now lunge the horse with side-reins. The side-reins should be the same length, and they are attached to the front girth straps. To start with they should be so long that they have no effect on the horse's mouth beyond their weight alone.

Then, gradually as the days pass, the side-reins should be shortened, but never by more than one inch or one hole a day. For the first few days there will be virtually no contact, and the horse will trot around on the lunge with its nose stuck out. Gradually the horse will come to make light contact with the bit. On no account should the horse shorten its neck, or resist the bit by putting its tongue over it or by keeping its mouth open. If this happens the side-reins must be lengthened, and this part of its training taken a lot more slowly.

The side-reins are not clipped on to the bit until the horse is in the lunging area, and they are always tightened with the outside one being done before the inside one. Then the horse is immediately asked to move forwards. Otherwise the horse may rear and fall over backwards when it feels the restriction of the reins.

The horse should have light contact with the bit with a long neck, the nose lowered, and the back rounded with the hocks working well under him. The final length of the side-reins is reached when the horse's head and neck are in the desired position for a correctly trained horse. As soon as the horse stops work on the lunge the side-reins are immediately released.

Day 8

Mounting the horse

The first few times we get on the back of the horse we want someone to leg us up. An assistant is needed to hold the horse, to reassure it by talking quietly to it and by giving it mouthfuls of food. He or she then takes our leg and boosts us carefully on to the back of the horse so that we are lying across it. We don't sit up. Instead, we just slide off again after a few seconds. We do this once or twice more, and each time the horse is rewarded. Then, the next time we are legged up if the horse is fairly relaxed, we slowly sit up. We sit there quietly, tell the horse how clever it is, and the handler rewards it with food. Then the handler can take us for a little walk and lead us around on the horse for a minute or two. If the horse is uneasy; end the training session. Get off and reward the horse. Next day the horse will probably be more at ease.

However, if the horse is relatively happy about walking around with us on its back, we can try a *sitting* trot. A few minutes riding only the first day is enough. We then dismount (without using the stirrup), make much of the horse, and reward it with food.

In all our training of the horse we must listen to it, and not ask it to do things too soon or at the wrong time. This is only an outline or guide for breaking in a horse, and as all horses are individuals each one will need to be treated a little differently.

Day 9

Mounting via the stirrup

After the day's lunging session, we can again be legged up on to the back of the horse and led around at a walk and a trot for a few minutes longer than the previous day. By now the horse is probably quite happy about us being on its back, so we can think of mounting it from the stirrup.

The assistant holds the horse, reassures it, feeds it some grain or titbits, while we thump on the saddle, swing on the stirrups like we have been doing for the last few days, and if the horse says 'Okay' like we expect, we carefully mount via the stirrup. On no account must we stick our feet into the horse or take on the bit. The horse is then stroked and rewarded. The handler then leads us around the lunging area for a minute or two.

Day 10

Riding on our own

The horse is used to being led and doing what a handler

on the ground says. Now it has to learn to accept instructions from someone on its back instead. This is initially hard for the horse to understand.

The assistant leads horse and rider around in a large circle on the lunge rein or a leading rope, but gradually tries to disassociate himself from the horse, while at the same time the rider tries to get the horse to understand what he wants by pushing the horse forward with his seat and back and squeezing gently with his legs to encourage it to do so. *Don't kick the horse!* As we have said before: force begets force! We want the horse to obey our instructions on the slightest command; not on gross and heavy actions. Besides, why should an untrained horse imagine a kick in the ribs is to make him move forwards? Why shouldn't he go upwards instead?

The horse is ridden with two hands, correct riding aids – especially from the back and legs – and verbal commands to help it to understand. The contact on the bit is light, even, and consistent. The assistant actively leads the horse forward only when it is necessary, and tries to be as unobtrusive as possible.

We ride the horse on the lunge area for no more than ten minutes. We want the horse to accept what we are doing without it becoming cross or bored. We walk circles, figures of eight, and serpentines, and always an equal amount of work in both directions so that the horse does not become unevenly balanced and muscled. The purpose of the serpentines is to teach the horse the aids or signals we are going to give it to turn. We want to be particularly careful that we use our legs and back properly and don't attempt to turn the horse only with the rein.

We finish the day's ride with about half a minute's rising trot on each diagonal. The horse is then given a caress and cuddle and rewarded.

Day 11

Mounting without assistance

The next day, after the initial lunging period, the horse can probably be mounted without any help. We need to swing our weight from the stirrup leathers first, like we have been doing over the last few days, to remind the horse what we are going to do so that it won't take fright. It is also a good idea to give the horse a handful of oats now, and the next few times we mount it. If the horse has a tendency to move off while we mount, we need to stop this right at the beginning before it becomes a bad habit. If we are careful and gentle with the horse and it still walks off, it is a good idea to mount it where it is more difficult for it to do so. Perhaps in the usual grooming spot where it is used to being tied-up, or in front of a fence or gate. If the horse is very bad it may be a good idea to get the horse used to being mounted while it is tied up. The rider can then just lean forward and unclip the horse from the rope when he wants the horse to move off.

The horse is again walked on the lunge area through circles, figures of eight, and a serpentine or two. It is also trotted on a large circle. It may or may not have got the idea of moving forward without someone to lead it, but by the following day it probably will.

Day 12

Riding without assistance

We can now be more adventurous and ride the horse further afield; perhaps around the house, through the different yards, and in the nearest paddocks – providing that the horse will not be worried by other livestock. For the most part we walk, but we can also trot a little. We do a rising trot, as a sitting trot is too hard on a young horse.

Day 13

'Whoa!'

'Whoa!' Where are the brakes? We haven't said anything about stopping the horse before now, because the horse has been likely to stop of its own accord; and our problem has been more in trying to teach the horse to move forwards. The horse must have impulsion; and trying to teach the horse 'stop' and 'go' at the same time is confusing and not very constructive.

Now that the horse understands walking and trotting with us on its back, it is time to teach it to 'whoa!'. We find it best to give the horse this lesson in the lunging area, and to only halt the horse several times.

We need to be careful not to halt the horse abruptly, but ask for a smooth transition to a halt by the correct use of back, legs, and reins. We also help the horse to understand by giving it the verbal command 'whoa!'.

Day 14

Exploration

We can now start riding the horse a little further from home, perhaps with a companion horse to keep our novice relaxed and happy. The better we can ride, the more we can help the horse to move properly, and the better will be the horse's mouth which we are also creating (or else ruining) day by day. However, we must remember that we are riding a novice horse, and we must not ask too much of it.

Day 15

Cantering

We feel that it is safer and creates less anxiety in the horse (and us) if it learns to walk, trot, and to slow down and stop, before we start cantering. A cantering horse is likely to get a lot more excited, and so is likely to pay less attention to us and what we want it to do.

It's easiest to teach a horse to canter in the company of another horse, on a straight line or on a huge circle, and where there is lots of space. It is not until a horse has learnt to canter well, and with some collection, that it can canter around a standard size manège without flying off at the corners!

Right from the beginning we are careful that we work the horse evenly on both sides, and make sure that we don't canter more on one lead than the other. Although at the start we are cantering the horse in a straight line, we ask the horse to canter at the moment we have it correctly positioned to naturally canter on the lead we are asking for. In other words, we actually commence to canter on the circle, but continue in a straight line. At first the horse may be reluctant to canter even a hundred metres without breaking back to a trot or changing legs, and it is not until it becomes proficient at cantering on both leads without breaking pace that we commence asking for more collection and cantering on a circle.

Day 16

Progress

By now our horse is virtually broken in. However, we must remember that our horse, being a three-year-old, is still really a baby and should not be worked hard or for long periods until it is at least four or five years old. So we only work the horse for a short period each day, such as twenty or thirty minutes, and if we wish to go further afield it should be an easy ride and for no more than an hour.

How should we use our time exercising the horse?

Day 17

Lunging

It is no longer necessary to lunge the horse every day

before it is ridden, although it may be advisable to do so if the rider's hands alone are not good enough to achieve a reasonable position of the horse's head.

Schooling

We also need to consider schooling. Probably nothing has the potential to be as creative or as destructive to the riding horse as schooling. Good and considerate schooling can make a horse a delight to ride: poor and inconsiderate schooling can totally ruin a horse's paces and destroy its mind through sheer mind-boggling boredom!

If we ride in the company of other horses, our horse will tolerate schooling on an arena with greater equanimity. Even so, ten minutes schooling should be the upper limit if we don't want to make our horse cross and bored and limit its abilities in other ways.

Riding for enjoyment

The way to achieve the benefits of schooling a horse without the disadvantages or risks, is to school the horse without it knowing!

The horse needs mental stimulation. It needs change and variety: it needs to go on doing new things, seeing new things, and learning new things. Otherwise we cannot expect to have a well-behaved and competent riding horse.

So we try to school the horse a little each day, and give it variety in its riding. We do a lot of our riding on unmade country roads, the grassy verges, and trails through the bush. We always ride as well as we can to help the horse; and we trot an equal amount on both diagonals, and canter an equal amount with both leads, so the horse is equally strong and balanced on both sides. We go where the road invites, where the path lies open, and where it will be fun. And when we come to some space, like a picnic ground or a clearing in the bush, we spend several minutes schooling the horse on the circle, and then we ride off again while the horse is still happy and alert.

Then, at the next space we come to we may do a little more circle work, so that by the end of the ride we have incorporated ten minutes satisfactory schooling into a pleasant ride for both ourselves and the horse.

Riding on the road

An experienced companion horse should go with our horse when it first starts working out on the road, to reassure it by its presence, to act as a shield between it and the traffic, and to teach the novice to accept the traffic without shying.

A companion horse is also very helpful in teaching a novice to do other things it may not have done before, like jumping up and down embankments, crossing wooden bridges and streams, and ignoring cows and sheep.

By the end of the month, the horse should be going so well for us that we feel really happy to have created such a successful partnership, and to have made such a good riding horse.

11

MAKING YOUR HORSE SICK

More horses get sick or injured during the weekend or when we are on holidays than at any other time: they come into greater contact with people!

Even if the care and management of our horse covers all its needs, so that it is happy and healthy – beware the weekend! Despite our best efforts, horses are frequently beset by troubles which we all too often unwittingly initiate ourselves.

Frequently these troubles are caused by us accepting the presence of horses around us as if they were a natural adjunct to our modern and machine-orientated lives. Whereas in fact, the horse is very much the same as it was in the Bronze Age – at least from an internal point of view regarding the horse's metabolism, digestive system, and temperament. So domestication of the horse brings with it a number of risks to the horse that we do not normally think about – risks which come from us imposing a way of life upon the horse that is unnatural to it and foreign to its evolutionary heritage.

Fifty million years ago, in the Eocene epoch, the horse was a small animal called *Eohippus* and stood only four hands high.[33] It was a many-toed animal, which gave it a better foothold in the soft ground of the vast inland swamps where it lived. Grasses did not exist then, and horses' teeth were only suitable for eating the soft foliage on which the horse browsed. Due to its small size, it could easily be caught and eaten by the large mammalian carnivores that had also come into existence, and which were many times larger than it. The horse's only defence was its instinct for fear and flight.

As the millions of years passed, horses slowly became bigger. Bigger horses had a better chance of outrunning their predators, and so had a higher survival rate. By twenty million years ago, in the Miocene epoch, the horse had grown to nearly ten hands in height. The climate and the ground were now drier, and the horse's feet were becoming more suitable for running fast on firm ground. It now had three rather than four toes on its front limbs, and the third digit – now the central remaining toe – became increasingly larger. The marshy forested country had receded, and grass covered large open prairies. To cope with this changing diet the horse's teeth had slowly been changing too. From the low-crowned, non-grinding molars of the earliest horses, teeth had become higher crowned and with the serrated structure typical of those in the modern horse.

The horse's digestive system also had to adapt to cope with the more fibrous food; and those lines of horses whose digestive system failed to slowly adapt through hundreds of thousands of years of eating a diet of grass failed to flourish.

By the Pliocene period, ten million years ago, the horse now called *Pliohippus* was still only ten hands high. However, it now looked like a horse. It had a mane; a horse-shaped head, body, and legs; its third digit had grown wider and longer forming a hoof, and the remaining toes had disappeared.

Unfortunately for *Pliohippus*, it was still a favourite dinner for the carnivores which pursued it, such as the sabre-toothed tiger.

Then, one million years ago, the terrors of the horse were further increased by the emergence of man who had sufficiently evolved to use tools and to hunt horses for food. Bones found in the rubbish piles of cave-dwelling Stone Age men indicate that the horse was a staple part of man's diet.

By the beginning of historic times the horse's best defence against danger was still its instinct to shy and gallop away from every unexpected sight, sound, or movement around it; and the horses that survived tended to be the fastest, and so consequently were also the tallest. Man and other predators were more successful at killing the smaller and slower horses, and so by this crude process of selection boosted the height of the tallest horses to about thirteen and a half hands.

Nowadays, because of our intervention, most horses do not roam over vast tracts of land. This presents the modern horse with two dangers it did not face in the past: fencing, and heavy infestation by internal parasites.

We put a fence around our horse so that we can keep possession of it; and nearly all fencing carries some degree of risk to a horse, often because of the horse's well-developed instinct to jump first and to look later. A badly frightened horse may forget about fencing: it has no natural instinct to avoid it. Yet wire fencing can cut skin, muscle, and tendons; while post and rails can shatter bones.

Come the weekend, and we may decide it is time to move our horse to a better pasture. We are in a hurry. We forget that our horse will need to be introduced carefully to the strange horses in the new paddock so that they accept each other. We turn our horse loose, and a more aggressive horse promptly chases it into the fence!

Fencing not only poses the threat of injury to the horse, but by limiting the horse's grazing to a smaller area than it would choose itself, makes the horses in the paddock graze over the same grass again and again. This means that the horse has a much greater risk than it would in the wild of eating grass that has been contaminated by the larvae of internal parasites from its own manure or that of other horses. We may think that this is of no consequence due to our regular use of modern horse wormers, but unfortunately wormers don't manage to destroy one hundred per cent of worms.

So when we move horses around from one area to another area where there are horses, we can increase the risk of our horse being infected with parasitic larvae or even being infected with a different variety of worms that do not exist in its home territory.

There are also other risks to the modern horse that it did not suffer before its domestication: they concern having to carry our weight, problems with feed, and colic and psychological stress.

The horse has not been designed to carry our weight. Evolution designed the horse to only carry itself and to run fast.

Initially horses were virtually unknown to the earliest ancient civilisations. The City States of Mesopotamia, the Indus Valley, and Egypt flourished for hundreds of years without the help of horses. Before 2000 BC, the Mesopotamian army used onagers, a variety of Asian wild ass, to draw chariots of élite soldiers into battle. However, this all changed shortly after 2000 BC. Illiterate barbarians using horses and chariots overthrew these great civilisations, and established chariots drawn by

> horses as the major advantage for successful warfare until the first millenium BC.
>
> It seems that the early horses did not have the strength or stamina for carrying a grown man – although people would not have been nearly as large nor as heavy as us. Around 2800 years ago, Assyrian warriors mounted on horseback had to lead a spare horse; and Herodotus recorded that as recently as 2500 years ago there were horses not strong enough to carry men, but when they were harnessed to chariots they were as fast as all others.
>
> However, when larger numbers of stronger riding horses became available, the greater manoeuvrability of cavalry quickly displaced the more cumbersome chariotry on the battlefields. From then on the destiny of many nations rode on the backs of horses into battle. Nevertheless, the fact remains that only a mature horse can carry our weight.

We know horses frequently break down when they are ridden too young. The Thoroughbred horse industry injures and destroys huge numbers of horses due to ignorant and greedy owners having high hopes of winning races for two-year-olds! The horse's immature leg joints, bones, tendons, and ligaments are most at risk, but back problems are common too. Skeletons of deceased race-horses sometimes show vertebrae that have become fused together from carrying weight when they were too young. So, if we've got any sense, we don't ride a horse when it is too young – irrespective of how big and strong it looks. Additionally, we wait until a horse is at least four years old or even older before we start asking much work of it or expecting it to jump even low obstacles.

It's fun on our holidays to ride with other people. However, we may unexpectedly find ourselves riding our horse harder or further than we had at first intended, perhaps because we are enjoying ourselves and we want to ride longer, or perhaps because we are in the company of fitter horses. Sound and mature horses can also break down if they are ridden too hard or too fast, especially if they have not been carefully conditioned prior to such work.

The horse's feed also presents a large area for potential problems. Most horses now eat quite differently than they did during millions of years of evolution. This has obvious disadvantages.

> The horse's digestive system and metabolism have been established for at least twenty million years to cope efficiently with a diet of grass. The horse has not been designed to digest and metabolise grain. However, we have in the last few hundred years made the horse unnaturally large and now we have to feed it grain to sustain it.
>
> Modern film makers persist in making us believe that horses have always been tall. In the world of celluloid fantasy the rulers of every country, from the earliest civilisations onwards, have sat high and ridden fast on the backs of tall and speedy Thoroughbreds – horses which were developed by horse breeders of the eighteenth century from a foundation stock of considerably smaller horses.
>
> We can see from sculptures and engravings made in ancient times that the small horse was universal to the ancient horse-using civilisations, regardless of how mighty or powerful the ruler was. So, in the first thousand years before Christ, armies with horse-drawn chariots and mounted warriors were busy changing the ownership of the world – all with horses rarely over thirteen and a half hands in height!
>
> Even during the time of Henry VIII (1491–1547), which was the period when armour reached its heaviest, British horses were rarely over thirteen hands. Henry

> VIII feared that 'the breed of good strong horses may die out' and decreed that landowners had to breed horses of at least thirteen hands in height!
>
> It was the desire of the British royalty and aristocracy to win horse races, which brought about the rapid development of the Thoroughbred in the first half of the eighteenth century. Selective breeding for speed caused a considerable increase in the size of many horses. In the same way, selective breeding in much more recent times, has established many other breeds of horse.

The large horse is not a product of nature, it is man-made. Consequently it requires grain to provide enough energy to sustain it, and even larger amounts of grain if it is in work.

Mismanaging the correct feeding of grain to a horse can give it many problems including founder, azoturia, splints, and demineralisation of the bones.

> In the earliest book on horsemanship, which was written by Xenophon about 2400 years ago, only a few hundred years after the horse was first domesticated, Xenophon mentions problems created by feeding grain. He refers to these ills in such an offhand way that we are led to presume that grain has caused the horse various troubles since its earliest use.
>
> Xenophon says: 'A secure stable is a good thing, not only to prevent the stealing of grain, but also because you can easily tell when the horse refused his feed. Observing this, you may know either . . . that he has been overworked and wants rest, or that barley surfeit or some other disease is coming on'.[34]

These days horses can still suffer from excessive grain, because their bodies are still designed for a diet made exclusively of grass.

There are also problems with feed and water in relation to exercising a horse that the horse would not face in the wild. We have to be careful not to feed or water a horse before it cools down, and not to water it immediately after it has eaten grain, or else we may give it colic.

Colic is one of the most subtle and complex ailments of the modern horse: it is also its greatest killer. People are frequently the direct or indirect cause of colic, so it would not have been very common in prehistoric times.

When we talk about 'colic' we actually mean abdominal pain. We recognise that a horse has colic when it appears ill at ease and keeps turning its head to look at its side. Or else it may paw the ground, kick up at its abdomen, get up and down, or roll. The horse may even rest in an unusual position, like upside down with all four feet in the air or sitting on its haunches like a dog. It may also try and urinate repeatedly.

Although colic is a sign of many conditions, for example, a mare that is going to foal is likely to show colicky signs beforehand, we normally associate colic with problems that affect the intestinal tract. These problems can be physical or psychological.

There are many physical causes for colic. The intestines may have suffered damage due to the ravages of internal parasites. The intestines may be impacted or blocked due to the horse eating rubbish or junk that has been left lying around, or eating other foreign matter like sand or nails. Horses that do eat such things are frequently bored or hungry. Or the horse may be suffering from gas distention due to defective feed and incorrect feeding methods. Gas distention doesn't sound like a serious problem, but it can be if it causes the bowel to twist in the same way that a child's balloon can be twisted into two smaller balloons. Many horses die of a twisted bowel because it can only be untwisted by surgical intervention.

However, the chances of getting colic are considerably reduced with good care of the horse. The horse needs to be on a good worming programme, and paddocks should not be overstocked. Additionally, paddocks ought to be rested periodically for two months so that any parasitic larvae die. The horse's feed must be of good quality, sufficient for the horse, and the horse should be fed regularly. The horse will also need adequate hay or grass to chew; otherwise it is more likely to eat sticks, stones, and other foreign objects. Pastures need to be kept clean of rubbish, rope, hay bands, and so on, otherwise the horse may chew and swallow them. Also, abundant fresh water should always be available.

Exercise of the horse ought to be appropriate to its fitness and condition. It should not be allowed to get dehydrated or suffer from electrolyte loss. A very hot horse must be allowed to cool down before it is given free access to water; and grain should not be fed to a hot or exhausted horse, or before the horse has had a chance to drink. However, even some of the best kept horses still get colic.

Even if horses have proper physical care there still remain two groups of horses who are particularly prone to colic: the aged and the anxious.

Aged horses are likely to get colic more easily than younger horses for a number of reasons. Nearly all horses do have some internal parasites despite regular worming treatments, and as a consequence an older horse has an increased chance to have some partial damage to the blood supply to the intestines. Additionally, the intestines of an aged horse are likely to be less resiliant and active, which will predispose the horse to colic, especially if it doesn't eat regularly or it swallows its food without chewing it properly. Again, old horses are more likely than younger ones to not chew their food properly because they are more likely to have bad teeth. The fact that the intestines of old horses tend to be more sluggish than younger ones also makes them more likely to get colic if they are not regularly exercised. The aged horse walking around the paddock grazing here and there, is at considerably less risk than the elderly yarded or stabled horse that is not exercised, because exercise stimulates the intestines.

Anxious horses are prone to colic. This occurs because when a horse becomes overanxious or stressed its brain cannot integrate or cope with the number of nervous impulses it is receiving. As a consequence, the horse's nervous system not only remains stimulated and liable to overreact to minor stimuli, but it may also stimulate unwanted reactions that control various bodily functions. So with an anxious horse, any extra stress may be enough to cause the horse's nervous system to overreact and affect the intestines causing colic.

Madam's family were an anxious lot. Madam herself displayed her anxiety quite clearly whenever some part of her daily routine was disrupted. She would stand on three legs, holding the fourth, a forelimb, up high under her chest, as if it were tied there with an invisible rope.

One evening, unexpected visitors descended on the stud farm, and by the time they had been entertained and sent home, the mares who lived out in the paddock were still unfed. All the mares had given up hope of getting supper that night and had wandered off to eat the pastures; except for Madam. She had built up so much anxiety waiting for her customary feed, that she had developed colic. When supper eventually arrived, she was too distressed to eat. Instead she put her head in her owner's hands and said, 'I hurt!' The owner realised what had happened, and with lots of reassurance, and some especially attractive food, the mare rapidly recovered.

As we have mentioned earlier, there are many things that can make a horse anxious, and if we further stress an anxious horse by neglecting its needs or breaking a daily habit, we may find that we have induced colic.

However, it is not only the horse with an anxious temperament that is at risk from colic, but also the horse that has *developed* a chronically anxious personality due to poor handling.

Hamar was an overdisciplined, underrewarded, highly-anxious Arabian stallion, who in his later years changed hands a number of times; with the result that when he eventually accepted his latest owner he became inordinately dependent upon her. Hamar was so anxious that he virtually forgot to eat unless a smorgasbord of hay bags filled with different kinds of hay were hung all around him.

One morning, unexpected visitors arrived for breakfast, so by the time Hamar's owner had arrived at the stable to replenish the hay bags, which were mostly almost full, Hamar was prostrate with colic. This sequence of events was repeated many times during the following weeks: visitors disrupted the timetable and Hamar got colic. Eventually, the habit of a fairly precise schedule was broken, and Hamar accepted greater flexibility in the day's events.

We've described how an accumulation of anxiety can cause colic in a horse: the horse that is already chronically anxious because of temperament or bad handling is then stressed by something else and becomes sick. So it follows that colic can also occur if a horse suffers a number of stresses at the same time. Stress can add up until the animal can no longer cope.

'Ron' had a two-year-old gelding that he had put out in the back paddock 'to grow'. He didn't have much contact with the horse except to worm it occasionally.

One day, when he was walking through the paddock to check another horse, he noticed that the gelding had cut its leg. Although the wound wasn't bad, it did require a few stitches. Without more ado he brought the horse in and put it in a yard by itself to wait for the vet.

The gelding was distressed and anxious at being separated from its friends, and within thirty minutes was prostrate on the ground with colic. Ron was almost a stranger to his horse and could offer it no reassurance; neither did he think of bringing in a companion horse which would have been a comfort for it. By the time the vet arrived it was too late.

Horses who suffer the stress of being hurt, together with the additional stress of being deprived of their companion or companions, are subject to colic if they are not used to being handled and gaining reassurance from people. This may explain why sometimes a horse may suffer the most horrendous injuries, yet survive the accident and its convalescence without the slightest sign of colic; whereas another, perhaps a full brother or sister, may get only slightly hurt, yet when brought in for treatment will promptly develop colic of great severity.

Sometimes people impose so much physical stress upon a horse that, when it does get colic, its chances of survival are extremely low.

'Clive' had turned his horses out in a large paddock for the winter. 'They deserve a rest!' he said. However, grass doesn't grow when it's cold; and he didn't give them any hay or grain, nor rugs nor shelter. 'They'll be right', he said. 'No worries!'

It was an ordinary winter: cold. The horses began to look poorer and poorer. They weren't exactly wormy, and they weren't exactly starved, but they were cold. Then it began to rain and rain, and the horses began to shiver.

The following week Clive bewailed his bad luck, that some of his best horses had died, to all who would listen.

'It was worms!' said the vet. 'It was lack of feed!' said the manager of the grain store. 'It was lack of warmth!' said the rug-maker.

'No, no!' remonstrated Clive. 'It was colic!'

However, they were all right. The stress from each problem had combined to form an insupportable load. Colic and death were the outcome.

Once a horse gets colic, irrespective of the cause, it can rapidly get worse without reassurance, or distraction, or painkillers. Pain feeds on pain!

Some colics that occur will be fatal irrespective of how they are managed, due to factors that cannot be reversed, such as arterial damage causing degeneration of the bowel. However, many other colics have an unnecessarily fatal outcome.

Our best defences against fatal colics are good care and management of the horse, knowing the normal behaviour of our horse, being aware that the horse has abdominal pain before it is too bad, and knowing what psychological help we can offer.

We actually want to be able to know that the horse is unwell before its pain escalates to the stage that it is rolling and is very distressed. If we realise a horse has colic in its earliest stages we can possibly effect a cure in twenty or thirty minutes; providing of course that there isn't a death-inducing condition present already.

Early signs of colic can sometimes be seen in the unusual behaviour of our horses. The horse may sit down at an unusual time, or it may be the only one in a group sitting down. The horse may sit or lie in an unusual position, which is an indication of it trying to relieve pain. The horse may be reluctant to eat at a meal time, and it may even walk off or sit down instead. If the horse looks at its side occasionally, and not just the view behind it, it is time for action!

We give the horse some feed it may enjoy eating, like

good alfalfa hay or freshly cut oats or grass (not lawn clippings as they heat up too easily). If we can get the horse to settle down and eat, the battle is probably won. However, we don't feed grain, unless it is only a very small amount mixed with lots of bran and lucerne chaff and dampened, because it may add to the problem.

If other horses are going to be a nuisance, and we have to move the sick horse, we bring with it its favourite companion. The companion we keep nearby but on the other side of a fence. We don't put the sick horse in a strange yard or stable, but keep it in familiar surroundings.

We sit on the ground with the horse if it is lying down, and do our best to be calm and reassuring. Reassurance is an essential factor in trying to cure a horse with colic. It is amazing how many horses rapidly recover from an attack of colic if we sit with them and are calm and comforting; it is also equally amazing how fast a horse can deteriorate if we don't! The horse's anxiety about the pain increases the horse's perception of pain and worsens its condition.

If the horse shows no improvement, some distraction may help. We want to try and get the horse's mind off the pain. If the horse is standing up we may walk it around where there is something interesting to look at like other horses. We don't ride it or lunge it because that may hasten a fatal outcome. If the horse wants to sit or lie down we let it.

We also keep offering the horse some food. However, if our care and emotional support does not help (in most cases it will) and the horse gets worse, becoming more distressed and wanting to roll, we call the vetinarian if we have not already.

There is no hard and fast rule about not letting a horse with colic roll providing it is not frantic or hurting itself. There is evidently little danger of rolling causing a twisted intestine. However, if the horse is trying to throw itself on the ground for an energetic roll, it is possibly better to distract it with a walk.

Excessive walking can cause additional stress to the horse, especially if it is suffering from spasmodic colic and already overstimulated intestines. (In spasmodic colic intestinal rumblings can be heard and the horse may be passing manure or even have diarrhoea.) However, if the horse is showing signs of abdominal pain, but is not passing any manure and no abdominal sounds are heard (signs of an intestinal tract that is not functioning), walking can be helpful to stimulate normal intestinal activity.

Psychological help can certainly encourage a horse that hasn't got a pathological condition to make a rapid recovery. Reduction in the horse's anxiety can help relieve spasm in the intestines, so that accumulated gas is released, avoiding further build-up of gas which could lead to a twisted bowel.

If the horse is in pain, and making no signs of recovery, veterinary help should always be sought. The horse could have a serious blockage or other intestinal problems, and early detection and treatment will greatly increase the horse's chances of survival.

12

A HORSE OF OUR DREAMS

We may dream of owning a horse, yet when at last the dream eventuates we may find it is not as perfect as it had been in our imagination.

There are the many real problems of looking after a horse which involve time, work, thought, and money. However, there are also many other aspects to owning a horse that we may not have thought about at all. So sometimes when we have at long last managed to buy, breed, or borrow a horse, it does not live up to our expectations because it is quite unsuitable in some way.

The horse may not have the physical ability or the inclination to perform in the way we require. We may have too many expectations or unconscious desires to be fulfilled by the horse, or the temperament of the horse or the personality of the rider may be inadequate.

The horse must be physically suited to the form of work we want it to do, irrespective of whether it is to be used for casual riding or to perform in top competition.

Usually, when we buy a horse we have in mind some

specific purpose. We may want an eventer, a show jumper, a dressage horse, a show hack, or a children's pony, and so on; but whatever it is, the horse must have the physical properties for the task. Apart from looks, it must have the necessary size, conformation, soundness, and paces.

If we want a top show jumper, a pony is most unlikely to succeed, no matter how keen it is to jump, simply because it is too small when compared with larger horses who also have ability. In the same way, a tall horse is not very suitable for small children, because they are not only 'out-horsed', and the horse is more intimidating and further to fall from, but they also will miss out on lots of the pleasure children have riding bareback and the spontaneous fun of play that includes being able to jump on and off their horse without the necessity of a saddle.

Do we want a show horse? A potential show horse must be attractive and without obvious scars or blemishes, and it must have good conformation. Additionally, if the horse is to be shown in breed classes, it must have the features or type of that breed. A ridden show horse must also have good paces, not only to attract the judge's eye, but to enable the rider to ride to the best of their ability. The best show horses not only display a look of quality, but they also exhibit presence and charisma too.

Some horses need to be more sound than others. A Thoroughbred is likely to be an unwise investment as a racehorse, eventer, or jumper if he has faulty knees or off-set cannons, whereas the horse may be adequate for dressage or hacking. The horse must physically fit the task.

Even if the horse is physically suited to perform the type of work the owner has in mind, the horse may be temperamentally inadequate. It may not have the inclination for such an activity. It will then be totally up to us to use every bit of intelligence and understanding of horses that we possess to motivate the horse into a change of heart.

The need for the horse to have the motivation to perform

the work that we require of it is essential to the most successful performance horses: horses who have the ability and want to do something will do it better than those with ability but no inclination. So the horse needs to enjoy jumping to jump well; a good racehorse wants to win regardless of the physical cost to itself; a good child's pony takes pride in going well for its small rider when it could very easily dump the child on the ground instead; and a good hack or pony club mount may wish to perform well out of the trust and affection it feels for its owner. Needless to say, it is also up to us to foster a horse's inclination to work for us, and not to abuse or bore the horse so that we destroy all natural inclination.

Sometimes a horse may lack the inclination to do only one specific thing, like jumping, racing, or going through water. Or it may have some idiosyncrasy such as bucking, or rearing when excited, but in every other way may be a good horse. So a horse that is a failure for one person may be perfect for another who wishes to use it for another purpose, or who does not mind the horse's idiosyncrasy.

Gidget was a pony club horse. She was an unregistered horse and not especially beautiful, but she had perfect paces and a sweet and willing nature. In fact, she had no will at all to do her own thing; she simply wanted to do exactly what her rider asked – except jump!

'You must get a jumping horse, dear!' the pony club instructress would continually remonstrate with Gidget's owner. So she did. Gidget was sold and replaced by a beautiful-looking horse who would jump, but totally lacked virtues of pace or personality.

Consequently the girl ceased to enjoy riding. She sold the horse, and never rode again; although every now and then she wondered what had happened to Gidget.

Gidget eventually became the horse that fulfilled

someone else's dreams. Her beautiful paces and personality made her the perfect ride, the perfect friend, the perfect partner: a horse which for some people is beyond price!

A common problem with horses that can make all the difference between them being a pleasure to own and a source of misery is a refusal to be caught.

If a horse is worked without it receiving some reward in return, we are in essence conditioning the horse not to be caught. As a result there are many good riding horses who refuse to be caught. However, even the most difficult horses can learn to accept being caught, providing we always reward them with a meal just before they are released again.

Firedance had been made impossible to catch by her fear of being hurt and the absence of any reward. When she was bought for her previous owner as an eight-year-old she was beautiful, thin, afraid; and completely uncatchable. She was not foolish enough to accept a bucket of oats for the horrors that she thought still existed beyond the paddock gate. Pain caused by people had even physically left its scars on her – white spots in her chestnut coat where she had been girth and saddle galled, and heavy scarring around her mouth which had once dripped blood from the bits of the 'horse-breaker' and an early 'cowboy' owner.

So her new owner was forced to catch her by rounding her up on a horse and herding her into a yard. However, instead of something unpleasant happening to her, she was given a large meal of oats and alfalfa chaff, and was then released before she had quite finished the last mouthful.

The next day she had to be rounded up on horseback again, but this time when she saw the horse and rider walking across the paddock towards her, she walked up the hill and into the yard – where she was rewarded with food and a good scratch on her neck where she said she was particularly itchy.

On the third day the new owner walked on foot across the paddock and the horse walked into the yard, and on the fourth day the owner walked confidently up to the mare and caught her.

Firedance was always rewarded with food or a scratch when she was caught, and if she was ridden she was always fed before being turned out into the paddock with the other horses. She was never again difficult to catch.

Many horses indulge in bad behaviour, and a change in lifestyle and handling can sometimes make all the difference.

Donny was a gaunt and emaciated horse who belonged to a riding school. He possessed many vices and few virtues: it was only the brave who discovered that he had a canter which had the perfection of ease and serenity only found in dreams.

Donny always tried to bite or kick anyone who attempted to mount him, and if they did succeed, Donny would then treat them to a virtuoso performance of rearing and bucking. So people who went to ride at the riding school rapidly learnt never to accept Donny as a mount!

The horse was eventually sold to a kindly doctor for his sub-teenage children to ride. The doctor not knowing the worst of horses nor believing the worst of people, happily went back to work and left the children to 'enjoy' themselves.

The children, two sisters of eleven and twelve years, already had another rather recalcitrant pony, which they had learnt to ride through the well-tried system of 'the more you fall off the better rider you become' theory! So Donny's behaviour wasn't a great surprise to them.

Donny grew fat and sleek in his new home: and as his bad behaviour was ignored, he soon decided it wasn't worth the effort. He settled down and began to enjoy life as a valued member of the family.

Sometimes horses have absolutely no inclination to do what we want! These tend to be the most difficult horses. They can be strong-willed, cussed, and obstinate. However, if we correctly handle them, they can become top competition horses, but their lack of willingness in general excludes them from ever becoming real pleasure horses.

'Arnold' had 'a way' with horses, and as a result many rogue horses, or disasters created by other people were sent to him to train.

A part of Arnold's 'way' was to con the horse into enjoying itself: to re-channel some of the horse's negative emotions into more constructive behaviour by finding an activity that would help motivate the horse into being slightly more obliging.

As Arnold lived on a large country property, the horses were used in stock work. They were galloped over the hills, swum in the river, and cantered through the scrub jumping everything in sight.

One day Arnold was sent a well-bred Thoroughbred from another country property. It had been 'broken in' by another horse-breaker and now was mean, cranky, hated people, had a mouth like cast iron, and bucked incessantly.

Arnold rapidly discovered that he was a brilliant horse – at bucking! So he took him out with the other horses and riders who were enjoying themselves galloping crosscountry, and when he began to buck he discovered he was left behind – and bucked even harder in fury! But Arnold persisted, and after a few days the

> horse realised that if he wanted to be with the other horses there was no time to buck, he would have to gallop instead to keep up with them. He then discovered that galloping with the other horses was fun.
>
> Arnold, who was a country racehorse trainer, decided to take the horse to the races; and the horse used every bit of his innate aggression and fight to win. His negative characteristics were channelled into a useful direction. He won many races, and when he eventually retired, no one minded that he could not be ridden outside the racecourse. His owners felt he had earned the right to resume his early idyllic days of carefree life in the herd.

Although people usually buy a horse for some specific purpose, they frequently have other conscious or subconcious expectations of the horse too. Consequently, the more qualities or dimensions that are required of the horse, the harder it will be to satisfy the owner. Our personality and our abilities will determine what extra requirements will be essential to us.

In general, it is not much use having a horse who is a brilliant jumper or potential show horse if it refuses to be trailered to various competitions. A hack may be a very limited ride if it is afraid of traffic and won't go out by itself. In the same way a racehorse won't try and win if it is afraid of other horses, or a children's pony be much use if it hates children. The list of such possibilities is endless.

It is the subtler expectations a person may have of a horse that may make a very good horse fall far short of some people's dreams. These are expectations that fulfill some need of the owner's personality, and frequently involve the interaction of the person's personality and the horse's temperament.

An unsociable horse who will not be caught is unsuitable for someone who is looking for a friend and companion. Although the horse can be taught to be caught, it is not very likely to become affectionate and companionable no matter how motivated and loving a new owner may be.

An anxious horse that spooks and shies is unsuitable for a timid rider; such a partnership is likely to aggravate the deficiencies of both. In the same way, an unwilling or ill-behaved horse is unfitting for someone lacking in confidence, unless they are extremely highly motivated to help the horse towards an easier frame of mind.

> 'Elvie' was a teenage girl who had always been insecure, and lacked confidence, not only in doing things but also in relation to people.
>
> So she bought a horse, just a baby, ten months old. When the horse reached its third birthday Elvie had him broken in. The first time she rode him he bucked her off; but oddly for her, she did not give up. The horse meant too much to her, and so although she was terrified she courageously mounted him again – and he bucked her off again! And so it went on for a while, and eventually the horse stopped bucking and she stopped falling off; and they both learnt to enjoy going for rides together.
>
> What could have been a disaster, turned into a triumph; and Elvie's confidence got such a boost that it overflowed into the rest of her life, and somehow everything seemed much easier and happier than it had been before.

Some horses are gentle, placid, and slow. However, drifting peacefully and happily along in the sunshine is a characteristic quite unsuitable for a person whose mind suffers from chronic hurry. These peaceful horses, although they are obvious treasures to some, can drive others into a state of heartless fury, due to the difficulties they encounter getting much enthusiastic acceleration from their mount.

We obviously need to be careful not to buy a horse that reinforces less desirable aspects of our personality.

Moonraker was a very showy black gelding who had an impatient personality. He was always on the move, bossing other horses around the paddock, pawing the fence, banging at his stable door if he was shut in, or digging impatiently at the ground whenever he was tied up.

He was bought by a man who wanted him for stock work. On the man's farm there were many gates, and he expected the horse to stand still at each gate without him getting off so that he could manipulate the catch. However, Moonraker was too impatient to stand still, and became considerably agitated and upset when the farmer tried to make him; and the harder he tried, the angrier they both became.

Wisely, the farmer sold his horse and bought a farm bike, and Moonraker went to a new home where his impatience was accepted with tolerant good humour and at times was even valued. Moonraker's need to be continually on the move meant that he was an enthusiastic horse to ride; and as he didn't like stopping or waiting around, he seldom balked at any obstacle or jump out hunting or eventing, which were the forms of riding his new owner enjoyed most.

There are other problems, too, in buying our 'dream horse'. It may not live up to our expectations because it is different from how it appeared on the day we bought it.

These days many people are reasonably sophisticated about selling horses, and the horse is likely to be put up for sale at a time when it is at its very best. The horse is likely to be groomed and fed as if for a show, and worked every day for a number of weeks or longer. The horse may be at its peak. If we do not put so much work into the horse we may not be able to maintain its condition and performance.

Many horses are made more passive and controllable by

work and lack of feed. Sometimes difficult horses are worked very hard before they are put up for sale, so that they become tired, and their behaviour is at its best.

A horse's environment can also dramatically alter the horse's personality, in the same way that environment affects people. A horse that is continually stabled may be very excited, dancing on its toes, and full of presence when brought out; whereas the same horse kept in a paddock may be quiet and placid.

> Ming was a sleek black children's pony, who lived with some other ponies in a flat and treeless paddock, surrounded by factories, on the outskirts of the city. Despite her glistening coat she was an ill-assorted looking pony – seemingly representing every breed of horse in the one animal: the large body of a cob was set on short fine legs, and the long neck ended in a strange square head from which stared huge and lovely eyes.
>
> When a family who wanted a pony came to inspect her, they found a sad, depressed, spiritless little horse, who moved listlessly along with the young riders on her back. They never really knew why they took her home – it must have been because of her lovely eyes!
>
> From the moment Ming arrived at her new home in the hills, she was a changed horse. She stood on top of a hill sniffing the air and its smells of trees and grasses, and snorted in delight and excitement. Then she galloped off pigrooting, completely ignoring two ponies nearby, and joined the small group of Thoroughbreds who were grazing further away. She obviously believed that she was a Thoroughbred, although her aristocratic coat was the only clue! Never again was she a sad, depressed pony. She was a joyful, excitable Thoroughbred, requiring a rider to match!

If the horse has been prepared for sale by a more competent

rider than we are ourselves, and the horse tends to have an unwilling temperament; the horse will quickly discover our weaknesses and may become badly behaved.

There are other problems too in buying the ready-made 'dream horse'. Horses are usually upset by changes in their environment, irrespective of how well they are treated. Even if the new home is seemingly perfect, the horse may miss and even fret for its past companions, or owner, and it may take some days to settle down, and some months to settle in properly. The horse may be anxious and nervy for a while, and may even ignore its new owner, which obviously can be very disappointing. The new owner always has to work at winning the horse's trust and affection if they want to have a good relationship with it.

A frequent problem in buying a horse that appears to have all the virtues we want, is that it has a high chance of having some physical or behavioural problem, and that is why it is being sold.

> One hundred years ago, a knowledgeable horseman called General Tweedie, wrote a book about the Arabian horse in India.[35] Most of the horses he wrote about were for the British troops to ride and were bought from dealers in the Indian bazaars. After one such occasion of buying new horses, he relates how they had been on the march for some miles, when the hoof of one horse actually fell off! He says with some bewilderment that they never did discover how it had been fixed on in the first place!

Although these days no one is likely to engineer such an extreme deception, knowledgeable horse people can still be fooled into buying horses that are unsound in body or mind through the use of pain killers and tranquillisers.

It is much more likely that the horse will be satisfactory

from the point of view of soundness and behaviour if the owner has a genuine reason for selling it.

A family may have quite clearly outgrown their pony; a pony clubber may want a horse that is a better jumper; or a retired farmer may be selling his last and favourite stock horse.

Although we can buy a horse to satisfy some specific purpose, or simply to enjoy in casual riding, it is obvious that the horse that inevitably comes closest to our dreams will be one that we have shaped and made ourselves.

Additionally, understanding the horse helps us to develop a special friendship and empathy with it, so that we can successfully make an untutored horse into an educated one, or make a poor horse into a good one, or a good one into a better one. But even more than this we may find that we have created the 'once in a lifetime horse', the real 'dream horse', the one that answers some needs within us to such an extent that we know that we would never willing part with it at any price or under any compulsion!

NOTES

1 Adapted from: Plutarch, *The Lives of the Noble Grecians and Romans*, Trans. John Dryden, The Modern Library, New York, rpt, 1864

2 Podhajsky, Alois, *The Complete Training of Horse and Rider in the Principles of Classical Horsemanship*, Wilshire Book Company, California, 1973

3 Xenophon, 'On Horsemanship', *Minor Works*, Trans. J S Watson, George Bell & Sons, London, 1888

4 ibid.

5 Podhajsky, Alois, *The Complete Training of Horse and Rider in the Principles of Classical Horsemanship*, Wilshire Book Company, California, 1973

6 ibid.

7 ibid.

8 Wynmalen, Henry, *Horse Breeding and Stud Management*, J A Allen & Co Ltd, London, rpt, 1971

9 Clabby, John, *The Natural History of the Horse*, Weindenfeld and Nicolson, London, 1976

10 Blake, Henry, *Talking with Horses*, Souvenir Press, London, 1976

11 Blake, Henry, *Thinking with Horses*, Souvenir Press, London, 1977

12 Victorian Division of the Arabian Horse Society of Australia, Arabian Horse Seminar, Melbourne, 1981

13 Naviaux, James L, *Horses in Health and Disease*, Arco Publishing Company, Inc, New York, 1974

14 Riesen, Austin H, and Zilbert, Dale E, 'Behavioral Consequences of Variations in Early Sensory Environments', in Austin H Riesen (ed), *The Developmental Neuropsychology of Sensory Deprivation*, Academic Press, Inc, New York, 1975

15 Harlow, H F, and Harlow, M K, 'Learning to Love', *American Scientist*, 1966

16 Harlow, H F, and Harlow, M K, 'Effects of Various Mother–Infant Relationships on Rhesus Monkey Behaviors', in B M Foss (ed), *Determinants of Infant Behavior*, (Vol 4), Methuen, London, 1969

17 Konrad, K, and Melzak, Ronald, 'Novelty-Enchantment Effects Associated with Early Sensory-Social Isolation', in Austin H Riesen (ed), *The Developmental Neuropsychology of Sensory Deprivation*, Academic Press, Inc, 1975

18 ibid.

19 Mason, W A, 'The Effects of Social Restriction on the Behavior of Rhesus Monkeys: 1. Free Social Behavior', *Journal of Comparative and Physiological Psychology*, 1960

20 Miller, R E, Caul, W F, and Mirsky, I A, 'Communication of Affects Between Feral and Socially Isolated Monkeys', *Journal of Personality and Social Psychology*, 1967

21 Meares, Ainslie, *The Silver Years*, Greenhouse Publications, Melbourne, 1988

22 Plutchik, R, 'A Language for the Emotions', *Psychology Today*, Feb. 1980

23 Meares, Ainslie, *Life Without Stress*, Greenhouse Publications, Melbourne, 1987

24 Blake, Henry, *Thinking with Horses*, Souvenir Press, London, 1977

25 ibid.

26 Allport, Gordon, and Odbert, H S, 'Trait-Names: A Psycholexical Study', *Psychological Monographs*, 1936

27 Egyptian Stud Book, *History of the Royal Agricultural Society's Stud of Authentic Arabian Horses*, compiled by Dr Abdel A Ashoub, Cairo, 1948

28 Wentworth, Lady, *The Authentic Arabian Horse*, George Allen & Unwin Ltd, London, 1945

29 Egyptian Stud Book, *History of the Royal Agricultural Society's Stud of Authentic Arabian Horses*, compiled by Dr Abdel A Ashoub, Cairo, 1948

30 Mason, W A, 'The Effects of Social Restriction on the Behavior of Rhesus Monkeys: 1. Free Social Behavior', *Journal of Comparative and Physiological Psychology*, 1960

31 Tesio, Federico, *Breeding the Racehorse*, J A Allen & Co, London, 1958

32 Podhajsky, Alois, *The Complete Training of Horse and Rider in the Principles of Classical Horsemanship*, Wilshire Book Company, California, 1973

33 Roberts, M B V, *Biology: A Functional Approach*, Thomas Nelson & Sons Ltd, Surrey, 3rd ed, 1982

34 Xenophon, *The Art of Horsemanship*, Trans. Morris H Morgan, J A Allen & Co Ltd, London, 1962

35 Tweedie, Major-General W, *The Arabian Horse*, William Blackwood and Sons, Edinburgh, 1894

INDEX